• HBJ READING PROGRAM •

FANFARES

 LAUREATE EDITION

LEVEL 9

Bernice E. Cullinan
Roger C. Farr
W. Dorsey Hammond
Nancy L. Roser
Dorothy S. Strickland

HBJ HARCOURT BRACE JOVANOVICH, PUBLISHERS
Orlando   San Diego   Chicago   Dallas

Acknowledgments

For permission to reprint copyrighted material, grateful acknowledgment is made to the following sources:

Atheneum Publishers, a division of Macmillan, Inc.: "Until I Saw the Sea" from *I Feel the Same Way* by Lilian Moore. Copyright © 1967 by Lilian Moore.
Cynthia Overbeck Bix: Adapted from "Floaters, Poppers, and Parachutes: Seeds That Travel" (Retitled: "Floaters, Poppers, and Parachutes") by Cynthia Overbeck Bix. © 1984 by Cynthia Overbeck Bix.
Carolrhoda Books, Inc., 241 First Avenue North, Minneapolis, MN 55401: Adapted from *A Contest* by Sherry Neuwirth Payne. Copyright © 1982 by Carolrhoda Books, Inc.
Contemporary Books, Inc., Chicago, IL: "It Couldn't Be Done" from *The Collected Verse of Edgar A. Guest.* © 1934 by Contemporary Books, Inc.
Creative Arts Book Company: Adapted from *The Shoemaker's Gift,* interpreted by Lyndell Ludwig. Text copyright © by Lyndell Ludwig.
Delacorte Press: Adapted from *The Girl Who Knew It All* by Patricia Reilly Giff. Text copyright © 1979 by Patricia Reilly Giff.
Doubleday & Company, Inc.: "The Colors Live" from *Hailstones and Halibut Bones* by Mary O'Neill. Copyright © 1961 by Mary Le Duc O'Neill.
E. P. Dutton, a division of NAL Penguin Inc.: Adapted from *Do Not Open* by Brinton Turkle. Copyright © 1981 by Brinton Turkle.
Four Winds Press, an imprint of Macmillan Publishing Company: Adapted from *Maggie and the Pirate* by Ezra Jack Keats. Copyright © 1979 by Ezra Jack Keats. Adapted from *Ty's One-man Band* by Mildred Pitts Walter. Copyright © 1980 by Mildred Pitts Walter.
Harcourt Brace Jovanovich, Inc.: From *HBJ School Dictionary.* Copyright © 1985 by Harcourt Brace Jovanovich, Inc. From *The Community: Living in Our World* by Paul F. Brandwein and Nancy W. Bauer. From *HBJ Science,* Level Green, by Elizabeth K. Cooper et al. Copyright © 1985 by Harcourt Brace Jovanovich, Inc.
Harper & Row, Publishers, Inc.: Illustrations from pp. 4, 7, 18, and 24 in *Chanticler and the Fox* from *The Canterbury Tales* by Geoffrey Chaucer, adapted and illustrated by Barbara Cooney. Copyright © 1958 by Harper & Row, Publishers, Inc. Published by Thomas Y. Crowell. Complete text, abridged and adapted, and illustrations from *THE GREAT BLUENESS and Other Predicaments,* written and illustrated by Arnold Lobel. Copyright © 1968 by Arnold Lobel.

D. C. Heath and Company: "Trains at Night" from *The Packet* by Frances M. Frost.
The Instructor Publications, Inc., New York, NY 10017: "Face to Face" by Anita E. Posey and "My Star" by Marion Kennedy from *Poetry Place Anthology.* Copyright © 1983 by The Instructor Publications, Inc. Adapted from "Barbara Cooney's Award-winning Picture Books. . .'Make the World More Beautiful'" (Retitled: "Interview with Barbara Cooney") by Julia Smith from *Instructor* Magazine, March 1985. Copyright © 1985 by The Instructor Publications, Inc.
Lerner Publications Company, 241 First Avenue North, Minneapolis, MN 55401: Adapted from "Adrift in Space" (Retitled: "In Space") in *Adrift in Space and Other Stories* by George Zebrowski. Copyright © 1974 by Lerner Publications Company.
Lothrop, Lee & Shepard Books, a division of William Morrow & Company, Inc.: Adapted text, and illustrations from pp. 8, 9, 16, 17 and 27 in *Molly's Pilgrim* by Barbara Cohen, illustrated by Michael J. Deraney. Text copyright © 1983 by Barbara Cohen; illustrations copyright © 1983 by Michael J. Deraney.
Macmillan Publishing Company: Adapted from pp. 57–63 in *Away Goes Sally* by Elizabeth Coatsworth. Copyright 1934 by Macmillan Publishing Company, renewed 1962 by Elizabeth Coatsworth Beston. Adapted from *Galileo Galilei Space Pioneer* (Retitled: "Galileo") by Arthur S. Gregor, illustrated by James W. Williamson. Text copyright © 1965 by Arthur S. Gregor; illustrations copyright © 1965 by James W. Williamson. Adapted from pp. 18–42 in *Elisabeth, the Treasure Hunter* by Felice Holman, illustrated by Erik Blegvad. Text copyright © 1964 by Felice Holman; illustrations copyright © 1964 by Erik Blegvad.
McGraw-Hill Book Company: From pp. 91–92 and 116–117 in *Communities* by Leonard Martelli et al. Copyright © 1983 by McGraw-Hill, Inc.
William Morrow & Company, Inc.: Adapted from pp. 78-103 of "Ellen Rides Again" in *Ellen Tebbits* by Beverrly Cleary. Copyright © 1951 by Beverly Cleary. "Beauty" from *I Am a Pueblo Indian Girl* by E-Yeh-Shure'. Copyright 1939 by William Morrow & Company, Inc.; renewed 1967 by Louise Abeita Chiwiwi.
Russel & Volkening, Inc. as agents for Harry Hartwick: Adapted from pp. 32—57 in *The Runaway Ride of Old 88* by Harry Hartwick. Copyright © 1971 by Harry Hartwick. Published by Little, Brown and Company.
Silver Burdett Company: From pp. 40–41 and 45–47 in *Silver Burdett Science.* © 1984 by Silver Burdett Company.
Viking Penguin Inc.: Adapted from *Miss Rumphius,* story and pictures by Barbara Cooney. Copyright © 1982 by Barbara Cooney Porter. Illustrations from pp. 1, 8, 14 and 32 in *Ox-Cart Man* by Donald Hall, illustrated by Barbara Cooney. Illustrations copyright © 1979 by Barbara Cooney Porter.
Walker and Company: From p. 1 in *A First Look at Seashells* by Millicent E. Selsam and Joyce Hunt. Copyright © 1983 by Millicent E. Selsam and Joyce Hunt.
Albert Whitman & Company: Adapted from *My Dad Is Really Something* by Lois Osborn. Text © 1983 by Lois Osborn.

Contents

Unit 2
Portholes

Unit 3
Beauty

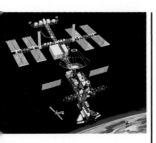

Unit 4
Milestones

Awards

The authors and illustrators of selections in this book have received the following awards either for their work in this book or for another of their works. The specific award is indicated under the medallion on the opening page of each award-winning selection.

The American Book Award
Irma Simonton Black Award
Boston Globe–Horn Book Award
Randolph Caldecott Honor Medal
Randolph Caldecott Medal
Lewis Carroll Shelf Award
Child Study Children's Book Committee at
   Bank Street College Award
Children's Book Showcase
Children's Choices
Christopher Award
Hans Christian Andersen Award
International Reading Association Children's Book
   Council Award
Coretta Scott King Award
National Council of Teachers of English Outstanding Trade Book
National Council of Teachers of English Award for Excellence
   in Poetry
National Jewish Book Award
John Newbery Honor Award
John Newbery Medal
New York Times Best Book for Children
New York Times Best Illustrated Children's Books
   of the Year
New York Times Outstanding Books
Parent's Choice Literature Award
Mark Twain Award
University of Southern Mississippi Medallion
Laura Ingalls Wilder Award

Unit 1

Passports

A passport is an important document that a person needs when traveling to certain countries. A passport guarantees that a traveler will be allowed to enter foreign lands. The word *passport* can also be used to mean an opportunity for something. For some people, learning can be a passport to success. An adventure can be a passport to change and to making new friends.

Not all of the characters in "Passports" travel, but they all learn from the adventures they have. Each one finds a passport or an opportunity for change in his or her life. Come aboard now and travel through the stories in this unit. As you read, try to decide how each character learns, grows, and changes as a person. Don't forget your passport!

The Drinking Gourd *by F. N. Monjo. Harper.* There once was a different kind of railroad called the "Underground Railroad." It helped people escape from slavery. Tommy's father is a member of this "railroad," and one night Tommy must help.

Kimako's Story *by June Jordan. Houghton.* When a neighbor asks Kimako to walk his big dog, she enjoys it so much that she plans to save for her own dog.

The Story of Paul Bunyan *by Barbara Emberley. Prentice.* This is a tall tale about the famous lumberjack who is as gentle as he is strong.

Aboard a Steam Locomotive: A Sketchbook *by Huck Scarry. Prentice.* You will learn a lot of information about steam trains from this book, which has many interesting drawings.

Alina: A Russian Girl Comes to Israel *by Mira Meir. Jewish Publication.* This is the story of a girl who moves from Russia to Israel. She feels out of place in her new country.

How My Parents Learned to Eat *by Ina R. Friedman. Houghton.* This book is about a girl and her family who eat with chopsticks one day and knives and forks the next. Her father is an American sailor who married a Japanese girl, and they practice each other's customs.

John Henry: An American Legend *by Ezra Jack Keats. Pantheon.* This is a tall tale about the man who was "born with a hammer in his hand." He challenges the new steam drill to a contest of power.

The Adventures of Marco Polo *by Demi. Holt.* This is a biography of the thirteenth-century explorer who spent seventeen years in Asia and became a friend of the emperor of China.

The Carp in the Bathtub *by Barbara Cohen. Lothrop.* Two children befriend and save a fish that their mother intends to cook for a very special holiday dinner.

The shoemaker's passport is an unusual piece of leather. What adventures does the shoe- maker have as he travels?

The Shoemaker's Gift

interpreted by Lyndell Ludwig

Many years ago, in a village in China, there lived a poor shoemaker. The shoemaker was skilled at mak- ing sandals and other footwear for the people in the village. One day the shoemaker found an unusual piece of leather. "What a fine piece of leather," he thought. "I will make a pair of hunting boots out of it."

The shoemaker worked hard on the boots. He worked in his spare time and often far into the quiet hours of the night.

When the boots were finished, his wife saw them and said, "What a handsome pair of boots! It would be a shame to sell them. You must take the boots and give them to the king."

6

The next day, the shoemaker started out toward the city where the king lived. The city was surrounded by a high wall. The shoemaker came to the main gate. When the guard who was watching at the gate saw the shoemaker, he blocked the shoemaker's way with his spear. "Halt!" said the guard to the shoemaker. "State your business or I cannot let you enter the city."

The shoemaker answered without a pause, "I have brought a present to give to the king."

The guard looked at the bundle the shoemaker was carrying. "When anyone gives the king a present and he accepts it," the guard said in a low voice, "the king always grants him something. If you will give me one-third of whatever the king gives you, I will let you go in." This did not seem right to the shoemaker, but he agreed, and the guard let him enter the city.

The shoemaker walked toward the palace. A second guard stood at the gate to the palace. When the shoemaker came to him, the guard stepped in front of him and blocked his way. "Halt!" he said. "State your business or you cannot enter the palace."

"I have a present to give the king," the shoemaker said.

8

The guard lowered his voice. "If you agree to give me one-third of whatever the king gives you, I will let you enter." Now the shoemaker thought that everyone in the city was a thief.

"All right, I will give you one-third of whatever the king gives me," he said. The second guard let the shoemaker enter the palace grounds.

The shoemaker walked toward the main hall. Just inside were two doors where a third guard watched. The guard stepped forward. "Halt!" he said. "State your business or I cannot let you in."

"I have come to give the king a present," the shoemaker said.

The guard lowered his voice to almost a whisper. "Not everyone can see the king," he said. "If you will promise to give me one-third of whatever the king gives you, I will let you go in."

The shoemaker answered without a pause. "I promise to give you one-third of whatever the king gives me." At once the third guard pulled open the doors.

The shoemaker knew that the three guards would take all of whatever the king might give him. Still, he entered the chambers of the king.

"Who are you?" asked the king.

"I am a village shoemaker. I made a pair of hunting boots and I have brought them here to give to you."

The king watched the shoemaker take out the hunting boots. Then the king tried the boots on and said, "I accept these boots. Now it is my turn to give you a gift."

The shoemaker said, "Would you, great king, order that one of your strongest guards give me ninety-nine blows with a hard wooden stick?"

"This is an unusual request," the king answered. He turned to his chief secretary and said, "I order that this shoemaker receive ninety-nine blows with a hard wooden stick."

The chief secretary led the shoemaker out of the king's chambers. The third guard was still on duty outside the two great doors. The shoemaker whispered to the guard, "Follow me, and I will see that you receive one-third of the king's gift."

At the palace entrance stood the second guard. The shoemaker bent toward him. "Follow me," he whispered. "I will see that you receive one-third of the king's gift."

When they reached the main gate to the city, the first guard stood watching outside. The shoemaker whispered, "Follow me, and I will see that you receive one-third of the gift the king has given me."

The little group walked a short distance and stopped outside the city gate. The shoemaker spoke. "Today I came to the city to give the king a present. I had to pass by these three guards. Each guard said he would let me pass only if I would agree to give him one-third of whatever the king gave me. I now request that the king's order be carried out. I request that one of the guards with a hard wooden stick strike each of the guards one-third of the ninety-nine blows."

The chief secretary spoke, "So this is how it is! By order of the king, each of you shall receive thirty-three blows."

A crowd was beginning to gather. "Long live the shoemaker! He has repaid those who tried to cheat him," they cried out.

The king heard the noise and sent a messenger to fetch the chief secretary. The secretary told him about how the three guards tried to cheat the shoemaker. The king ordered the shoemaker to be brought before him. When the shoemaker arrived the king said, "You did the right thing."

The shoemaker smiled and slowly backed away to leave. Since everyone leaving the king's presence had to keep his eyes lowered to the ground, the last thing the shoemaker saw of the king was the beautiful pair of hunting boots he had made with his own hands. The king was still wearing them.

1. What adventures did the shoemaker have because of the boots?

2. What lesson did the three guards learn?

3. How did the shoemaker pay the three guards part of his reward?

4. How did you feel when the chief secretary told the guards about their reward?

5. How did the author tell you that the king rewarded the shoemaker for the gift?

6. How do you think the three guards changed as a result of the lesson they learned?

Prewrite

A lot of things happened to the shoemaker after he left his village. What was the most exciting thing? How did the shoemaker handle the things that happened?

Draft

Choose one of the activities below:

1. Pretend that you are the shoemaker returning from your journey to see the king. Write a paragraph about what you might tell your wife about your journey and adventures.

2. Pretend that you are the shoemaker, and write a letter to your village friends about your adventures.

Revise

Read your work over to yourself and then to a classmate. Does it seem like something the shoemaker might write? Discuss some possible changes with a classmate and then revise your story.

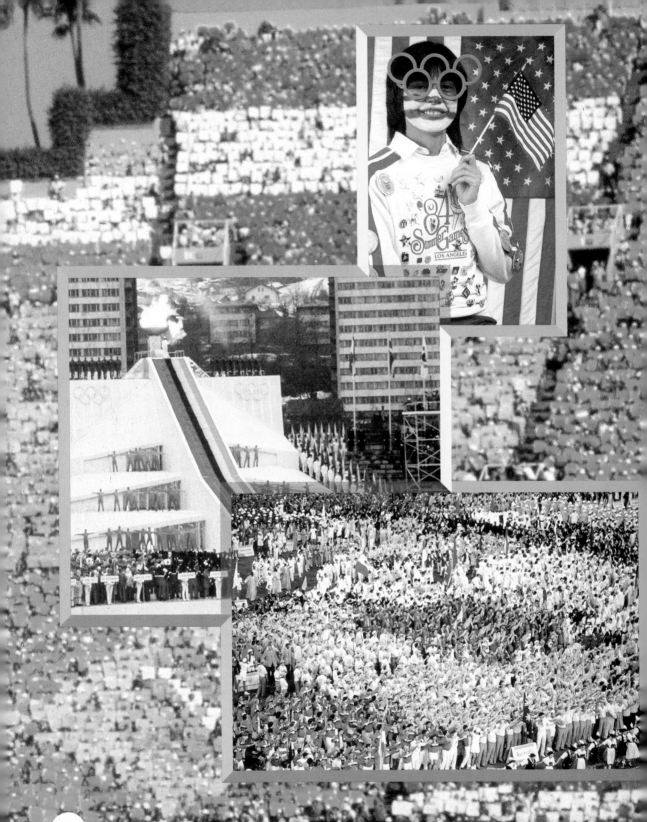

Face to Face

by Anita E. Posey

I'd like to go around the world
    And get a chance to see
The boys and girls of other lands
    And let them all see me.

I'd like to meet them face to face,
    And get to know their names.
I'd like to sit and talk with them
    And learn to play their games.

I'd like to visit in their homes,
    Their family life to share.
I'd like to taste the food they eat,
    And see the clothes they wear.

I'd like to get to know them well
    Before my journey's end;
For only when you know someone
    Can he become your friend.

And so, someday, I'd like to go
    Around the world and see
The boys and girls of other lands
    And let them all see me.

National Jewish Book Award

Molly is learning many things about her new country. What do Molly and the other children learn about the Pilgrims from a homework assignment?

Molly's Pilgrim

by Barbara Cohen

Molly is a little Jewish girl who came with her family from Russia to live in the United States. Molly did not like going to school because her classmates made fun of the way she spoke. Elizabeth usually laughed the most and said mean things to Molly.

The students in Molly's third-grade class had been reading about Pilgrims and the first Thanksgiving. Molly had never heard of Thanksgiving and had trouble reading the word. Her teacher, Miss Stickley, told Molly to read the story and it would explain the meaning of Thanksgiving. As the story begins, Molly has just come home from school.

When I got home, Mama said to me, just like always, "*Nu,*[1] *shaynkeit,*[2] do you have any homework?"

"I need a clothespin," I said.

"A clothespin? What kind of homework is a clothespin?"

"I have to make a doll out of it. A Pilgrim doll."

Mama frowned. "*Nu, Malkeleh,*[3] what's a Pilgrim?"

I searched for the words to explain "Pilgrim" to Mama. "Pilgrims came to this country from the other side," I said.

"Like us," Mama said.

That was true. "They came for religious freedom," I added. "They came so they could worship as they pleased."

---

[1] Nu [nū]: well, so
[2] shaynkeit [shān'kīt]: pretty one
[3] Malkeleh [mälk'el•ə]: from the Hebrew name Malkah

Mama's eyes lit up. She seemed to understand. "Do you have any other homework?" she asked.

"Yes," I said. "I have ten arithmetic problems. They're hard."

"Do them," she said, "and then go out to play. I'll make the doll for you. I'll make it tonight. It'll be ready for you in the morning."

"Just make sure it's a girl doll," I said.

"Naturally," Mama replied. "Who ever heard of a boy doll?"

I didn't bother to explain.

The next morning, when I sat down at the table for breakfast, the doll was at my place. Maybe she had started out as a clothespin, but you'd never have known it to look at her. Mama had covered the clothespin with cloth and stuffing. She had made hair out of dark brown yarn and she'd embroidered eyes, a nose, and a mouth on the face. She had dressed the doll in a long, full red skirt, tiny black felt boots, and a bright yellow high-necked blouse. She had covered the yarn hair with a yellow kerchief embroidered with red flowers.

"She's gorgeous, Mama," I managed to murmur.

Mama smiled, satisfied.

"But Mama," I added slowly, "she doesn't look like the Pilgrim woman in the picture in my reading book."

"No?" Mama said.

"She looks like you in that photograph you have that was taken when you were a girl."

Mama's smile turned into a laugh. "Of course. I did that on purpose."

"You did, Mama? Why?"

"What's a Pilgrim, *shaynkeit*?" Mama asked. "A Pilgrim is someone who came here from the other side to find freedom. That's me, Molly. I'm a Pilgrim!"

I was sure there was something wrong with what
Mama was saying. She was not the kind of Pilgrim Miss
Stickley or the reading book had been talking about. But it
was too late to make another doll now. All I could do was
take the only one I had to school with me.

Most of the dolls were out on the desks. I had carried
mine in a little paper bag. I put it inside my desk without
even taking it out of the bag.

The bell hadn't rung yet. Elizabeth and Hilda were
walking up and down the aisles, pointing to the dolls and
whispering. When they came to my desk, Elizabeth said
in a low voice, "Miss Stickley's going to be mad at you,
jolly Molly. She doesn't like people who don't do their
homework."

"I did it," I muttered.

"Well, then, let's see it."

I shook my head.

"You didn't do it," Elizabeth taunted. "You didn't, you
didn't."

I opened the desk and took out the paper bag. I closed
the desk and set the bag on top. Slowly, I pulled out the
doll.

"Oh, my goodness," Elizabeth sighed. "How can anyone be as dumb as you, jolly Molly? That's not a Pilgrim.
Miss Stickley is going to be really mad at you. Miss

Stickley's going to get you this time."

My face felt hot as fire. I looked down at my desk top.

The bell rang. Elizabeth and Hilda rushed to their seats. I shoved the doll back into my desk.

After morning exercises, Miss Stickley began to walk around the room, just as Elizabeth had. She looked at each one of the dolls. "Why Michael, what a magnificent headdress. Where did you find so many feathers? . . . Sally, she's lovely. Such an interesting face. . . . Such beautiful gray silk, Elizabeth. Yours is a very rich Pilgrim."

"I think she's the best so far," Elizabeth said.

"Well, she's very good," Miss Stickley allowed.

Then Miss Stickley came to me. Without looking up, I pulled my doll out of the desk.

I heard Elizabeth laugh out loud. "My goodness, Molly," she cried. "That's not a Pilgrim. That's some Russian or Polish person. What does a person like that have to do with Pilgrims?"

"She's very beautiful," Miss Stickley said. "Perhaps Molly just didn't understand."

I looked up at Miss Stickley. "Mama said . . ." I began.

Elizabeth giggled again.

Miss Stickley put her hand on my shoulder. "Tell me what your Mama said, Molly."

"This doll is dressed like Mama," I explained slowly. "Mama came to America for religious freedom, too. Mama said she's a Pilgrim."

Elizabeth hooted. She wasn't the only one.

Miss Stickley marched up to the front of the room. She turned and faced the class. "Listen to me, Elizabeth," she said in a loud voice. "Listen to me, all of you. Molly's mother *is* a Pilgrim. She's a modern Pilgrim. She came here, just like the Pilgrims long ago, so she could worship God in her own way, in peace and freedom." Miss Stickley stared at Elizabeth. "Elizabeth, do you know where the Pilgrims got the idea for Thanksgiving?"

"They just thought it up, Miss Stickley," Elizabeth said.

"No, Elizabeth," Miss Stickley replied. "They read in the Bible about the Jewish harvest holiday."

I knew that holiday, too. We called it Sukkos.[4]

"The Pilgrims got the idea for Thanksgiving from Jews like Molly and her mama." Miss Stickley marched down the aisle to my desk again. "May I have your doll for a while, Molly?"

"Sure," I said.

"I'm going to put this beautiful doll on my desk," Miss Stickley announced, "where everyone can see it all the

---

[4] Sukkos [sŏŏk'kəs]

time. It will remind us all that Pilgrims are still coming to America." She smiled at me. "I'd like to meet your mama, Molly. Please ask her to come to see me one day after school."

"Your doll is the most beautiful, Molly," Emma said. Emma sat next to me. "Your doll is the most beautiful one of all."

I nodded. "Yes," I said. "I know."

I decided if Miss Stickley actually invited her, it was all right for Mama to come to school. I decided something else, too. I decided it takes all kinds of Pilgrims to make a Thanksgiving.

1. What did Molly and the other children learn about Pilgrims?

2. Why did Miss Stickley put Molly's clothespin doll on her desk?

3. What did Molly understand about Thanksgiving at the end of the story?

4. How did you feel when Elizabeth laughed at Molly?

5. How did you know that Molly's mother understood the meaning of being a Pilgrim?

6. How do you think Molly changed as a result of what she learned?

Prewrite

Molly's mother came to America from another country. How do you think it feels to leave your home and live in a new country? What questions would you like to ask Molly's mother about moving to America?

Draft

Choose one of the activities below:

1. Pretend that you are a newspaper writer interviewing a person who is new to America. Make a list of questions you might ask and answer them as you think that person would.

2. Pretend that you are new to America. Write a letter to your family back home that describes what your new life in America is like. Tell how it feels to move to a new place.

Revise

Read what you have written. Do your questions and answers seem real? Does your letter describe your new life? Make any changes needed to make your work better.

Sequence

Look at the pictures below. Look for the order in
which things happen.

These pictures show a time sequence. Before Molly
can eat breakfast, she must first get the cereal, the
milk, a bowl, and a spoon. Then she must pour the
cereal into the bowl and add milk. When she has
done that, she is ready to begin eating. This is called
time order.

Recognizing time order is important in reading.
Writers often tell about events in the order in which
they happened. This helps the reader better understand what is being told.

Sometimes writers use clue words to signal time order. A few of these words are *then, when, now, noon, today, later, before, until, after, tomorrow,* and *at first.* Dates are also time clues. Sometimes dates are written as numerals: *1981.* Sometimes dates are written as words: *Fourth of July, April,* and *Tuesday.*

As you read the paragraph below, notice the dates and clue words that help you follow the time order.

No one knows exactly when people started wearing shoes. At first, people in the cold regions wore foot coverings to keep their feet warm. As early as 3700 B.C. people wore sandals in Egypt and Rome. Thousands of years ago people in China wore shoes with wooden soles. Later, in the 1500's, shoes were worn for fashion as well as protection. Today people still like to choose the shoes they wear for fashion.

The author used several time clues to help you understand the history of shoes. The dates written as numerals and the words *when, at first, later,* and *today* help you to understand the time order. In addition, the words *thousands of years ago* help you understand the time sequence.

Textbook Application:
Sequence in Social Studies

A social studies textbook can have many time clues. Read the following paragraphs. The sidenotes will help you find the time clues.

There are two time clues in this paragraph: *1865* and *then*. The date *1865* sets the time period. The word *then* shows what happened after 1865.

The date *1869* shows a time passage.

Instead of *1870*, the author wrote *One year later*.

The phrase *In the years that followed* shows more time passing.

1885 and the phrase *at this time* are two ways of showing the same time.

The first railroad came to Kansas City in <u>1865</u>. <u>Then</u> the river town began to grow into a big city. The railroad brought more people. It connected Kansas City with cities in the East. It carried mail and supplies back and forth quickly.

In <u>1869</u>, the Hannibal Bridge was built. It was the first railroad bridge across the Missouri River. This meant that railroad trains could go farther west. <u>One year later</u>, eight different railroads connected Kansas City with other places. <u>In the years that followed</u>, Kansas City became a marketplace for wheat. The wheat was grown on farms in the area. Railroads began bringing cattle from the West. Kansas City became a center for the cattle trade. In <u>1885</u>, the Kansas City stockyards were built. <u>At</u>

this time, flour mills and meat-packing plants were started. These industries are still important to Kansas City.

— *Communities*, McGraw-Hill

Read the next two paragraphs carefully to find the time order. No dates have been given.

For a long time, people walked wherever they went. Walking was their only means of transportation. Later, they may have ridden a horse. Or they might have ridden on a wagon pulled by a horse or other animal. They sent goods the same way. On water, they traveled in boats. They moved the boats with oars or sails.

Then, about 150 years ago, transportation began to change. Engines were used to move boats on water. They were used to pull loads on the ground. Because these engines were so heavy, they were put on iron tracks. This new means of transportation was called the railroad.

— *Communities*, McGraw-Hill

Time order helps you when you read. Dates tell when events happen. Other time clues also help.

Marco Polo went on a very long journey. What did he learn while he traveled? How did he share this information?

The Adventures of Marco Polo

by Peter Roop

As a young boy, Marco Polo often walked to the harbor in Venice,[1] Italy, to see the ships from faraway lands. He liked to watch the sailors in their colorful clothes unloading cargo such as silk from Damascus[2] and ivory from Africa. He also liked to smell the spices from the East.

---

[1] Venice [ven'is]
[2] Damascus [də•mas'kəs]

Marco's father, Niccolò,[3] and his uncle, Maffeo,[4] often traveled to far lands to buy spices. Just after Marco was born in 1254, Niccolò and Maffeo Polo traveled across Asia to the court of Kublai Khan,[5] the ruler of China. For seven years they lived at Kublai Khan's palace.

In 1269 Niccolò and Maffeo returned home and told Marco of their many adventures. These stories made Marco want to travel. When Niccolò and Maffeo decided to return to China, Marco begged to join them. He wanted to see the unusual people and places that his father and uncle had described.

When Marco was seventeen years old, the Polos sailed from Venice across the Mediterranean Sea. Then they traveled overland to China. Sometimes the road they wished to travel was blocked by fighting armies. Other times they had to go out of their way to pass around dangerous cities. When the Polos crossed the great Gobi[6] Desert in Mongolia,[7] they had to carry enough food and water to last for thirty days.

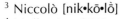

[3] Niccolò [nik•kō•lò]
[4] Maffeo [mə•fā'ō]
[5] Kublai Khan [kü'blə kän]
[6] Gobi [gō'bē]
[7] Mongolia [mon(g)•gō'lē•ə]

In western China the Polos climbed the Pamir[8] Mountains. Marco saw large sheep with curling horns over four feet long. Though Marco was not the first traveler to tell about these sheep, they have been named *Ovis Poli*[9] in honor of Marco.

Bad weather sometimes caused the Polos to stay in one town for months. Once when Marco got sick, they were

---

[8] Pamir [pə•mi(ə)r′]
[9] *Ovis Poli* [ō′vēs pō′lē]

forced to stay in one place for a year until he recovered. Marco was not bored while they waited because he spent his time learning the languages and customs of the people.

After three and a half years of hard and dangerous travel, the Polos finally reached Kublai Khan's court. Kublai Khan saw Marco and said, "He is welcome, and it pleases me much."

Marco found the court of the Great Khan amazing. When the ruler went hunting, he took 10,000 men with him. The palace had walls one mile long. Over 6,000 people could eat in the Khan's dinner hall. The Khan had a "pony express" system which carried messages across his huge empire.

Kublai Khan was curious about people and places. The Khan sent Marco throughout his empire as his "eyes and ears." When Marco traveled, he saw many new things. He saw books being printed on wooden blocks that had letters carved into them. As many as 5,000 books could be printed from one block. In Europe books were still being copied by hand.

While he traveled, Marco saw and learned about many things. He learned to use paper money. He watched wooden carts that were moved by sails roll down streets. He used a compass to help him find his way on the sea. He traveled on winding wooden roads built high on the slopes of steep mountains. He crossed marble bridges that ran across wide rivers.

Coal amazed Marco Polo. He had never seen a rock

that burned. He described coal as ". . . a black stone dug out of the mountains. When it is lit, it keeps the flame much better than wood." The Chinese used coal for cooking and heating.

After living in China for seventeen years, the Polos decided to return to Venice. Kublai Khan did not want the Polos to leave China but changed his mind when they agreed to travel with a Mongol princess to Persia.[10] In 1292 they set sail in Chinese junks. Marco found the junks amazing because they were made with many watertight sections. If a whale hit one section, the ship wouldn't sink. The other sections would help keep the junk afloat.

It took the Polos two years to get the princess safely to Persia. Finally, after having been gone for twenty-four years, the Polos reached home in 1295.

---

[10] Persia [pûr′zhə]

After Marco Polo had been home a few years, a writer, Rustichello,[11] wrote the story of Marco's travels. The book was called *A Description of the World*. Many people who read the book did not believe what Marco Polo described. However, one person did—Christopher Columbus. Nearly two hundred years after Marco Polo's trip to China, Columbus set sail to find the places Marco had described. Columbus never reached China but had many adventures of his own in discovering the New World.

Just before Marco Polo died, he was asked if he had been telling the truth about all of the things he had seen. Marco Polo replied, "I have not written down half of those things I saw." The things he did tell changed how people thought about the world.

---

[11] Rustichello [rus'tə•chel'ō]

37

1. What new things did Marco Polo learn as a result of his journey?

2. Why was the story of Marco Polo's travels important to the people of Venice in 1295?

3. Why was *A Description of the World* a good title for the book about Marco Polo's travels?

4. Would you have wanted to make the journey with the Polos? Explain your answer.

5. What in the story told you that people still thought about Marco Polo's adventures two hundred years after they happened?

6. How are people today able to learn about life in China from 1274 to 1296?

Think and Write

Prewrite

Marco Polo saw many things during his trips. He had a very interesting life. What do you think were the most important and exciting events in Marco's life? In what year did these events take place? Listed on the chart are some major events in Marco Polo's life and the dates on which they happened. Look back in the story and find the missing dates and events.

DATE	EVENT
1271	Marco left home.
1274	_____
_____	Marco left Kublai Khan.
1295	_____

Draft

Imagine that Marco Polo and Christopher Columbus lived during the same time. Pretend that you are Marco Polo answering a letter from Christopher Columbus in which he has asked you about your trip. Give details about your adventures. Use the chart to help you plan your answers and letter.

Revise

Does your letter include enough details about your adventures? Make necessary changes.

Story Elements

You know that stories and plays have characters. **Characters** are the people or animals the story is about. Some story characters are more important than others and are called **major characters.** In order to find the major characters in a story, you may want to ask yourself *who* the story is about.

In "The Shoemaker's Gift" the major character is the shoemaker. Other characters are the shoemaker's wife, the king, the guards, and many others.

Each story happens somewhere and at some time. The time and place of a story is called the **setting.** By asking yourself *where* and *when* the story happens, you are able to determine the setting of the story. The setting of "The Shoemaker's Gift" is in China, many years ago.

Usually the major character in a story has a **problem** that must be solved. The **solution** is the answer to the problem. In order to find the problem and the solution, ask yourself *what* the problem is and *how* it is solved. The shoemaker had to get past the guards in order to see the king.

Read the chart below.

MAJOR CHARACTER	Whom is the story about?	the shoemaker
SETTING	Where does it happen?	China, long ago
PROBLEM	What is the problem?	how to get past the guards
SOLUTION	How is it solved?	Shoemaker promises to give the guards one-third of whatever he gets as a present from the king.

Remember that a story is usually about one or more major characters in a specific setting. The characters have a problem and look for a solution.

Now decide upon the major character, the setting, the problem, and the solution for "Molly's Pilgrim."

Did you say that Molly is the major character? Did you identify that the setting is a classroom in the United States? Did you say that the children laughed at Molly's Pilgrim because it looked different? In your solution did you include the fact that Molly and her classmates learn that there are many kinds of Pilgrims?

As you read other stories, ask yourself the four questions to find the major character, the setting, the problem, and the solution.

A train ride turns into a dangerous and exciting adventure. What events take place on this ride?

The Runaway Ride of Old 88

by Harry Hartwick

Very carefully, Dave, the engineer, headed the freight train down the mountain. Then he let out the air brakes so the train could pick up a little speed. When the train had reached a faster speed, Dave tested the air brakes again. The brakes, which had been perfect only a moment ago, no longer worked! The train was starting to go faster.

Again he tried the brakes, but they still did not work. The train was gaining speed all the time. "No brakes!" Dave yelled. He signaled the brakemen and conductor to climb on top of the swaying cars and set the hand brakes.

As it went around the first curve, the train tried to leave the tracks—but held on. Looking back, Dave could see the conductor and two brakemen climb from the caboose onto the top of the cars. They ran along the catwalk trying to keep from being thrown off the moving cars.

When all the hand brakes had been tightened, Dave tested the air brakes again. Still the brakes were not working. Engine No. 88 was running free. There was no way to stop it. The train would just have to run till it reached the bottom of the mountain where the track leveled off or till it met something that stopped it. That something would probably be the night passenger train, No. 64.

Dave's orders called for No. 88 to head off onto a siding at Hamlin Crossing and let No. 64 go through. At this rate No. 88 would never be able to turn off the main line. The two trains could crash head-on unless they could get word to No. 64 before it reached Parkersville. To do this Dave would have to get a message to the station agent at Cantwell. Then the agent could send a message to Parkersville in time to get No. 64 off the main track.

The train gained speed as it ran down the track into Cantwell. Dave yelled to Spike, "Write a note—we'll throw it off—tell the agent to hold No. 64 at Parkersville!"

Spike nodded. He wrote a few words on a scrap of paper and wrapped it around a piece of coal.

As the train flew past the station, the agent stood on the platform. His mouth hung open in surprise.

Dave took the coal from Spike and held it up so the station agent could see it. Then he threw it very hard toward the station. The coal hit the ground and came apart. The paper blew along the platform where the station agent trapped it and picked it up. Dave could see the agent anxiously reading the note, and then running for the telegraph office door.

Telegraph poles were flying past the cab window in a steady blur. The wheels of the great train were pounding over the track. Dust was dancing on the floor of the swaying cab as the train flew through Hamlin Crossing, the place where they were to go onto a siding until No. 64 passed.

The wind beat at Dave's face as he anxiously stared at the track ahead. This curve was it! It led to Parkersville. If their note had worked, the track would be clear. If it hadn't, No. 64 would be coming right at them.

If they found No. 64 staring them in the face when the train rounded the bend, the crew would have to jump from the cab, and hope to save their lives that way. Dave called Spike to his side, and yelled to him, "Get ready to jump! Don't go till I tell you!"

Dave wanted to close his eyes as the train swept around the bend. He had to make himself look. Any moment he expected the crash to take place. He could see Spike standing just above the steps on his side of the cab, ready to jump. He got ready to jump himself.

As the train sped around the curve, Dave gave a happy cry. The track was clear! Far ahead, beyond the Parkersville station, he could see passenger train No. 64 sitting safely on the siding. A few seconds later, No. 88 roared past the passenger train.

Freight train No. 88 began to slow down as the track leveled off and began to climb into the mountains on the other side of Parkersville. Finally, three miles beyond the town, No. 88 stopped. It began to roll backward down toward the station. It passed the station, as a great cheer went up from the crowd that had gathered there. Then it rolled to a complete stop.

Dave turned and threw his arms around Spike, and for a moment they slapped each other on the back, shaking and laughing at the same time.

"They'll never get me on that engine again!" cried Spike, shaking his head.

They never did. Two weeks later Engine No. 88 was retired and put on a stretch of lonely track on the outside of the yards. There it sits to this day with its wheels rusted to the tracks and its bell hanging quietly.

1. What are two reasons the train ride was a dangerous adventure?

2. What problem did the brakes cause when they no longer worked?

3. Why did the train slow down and finally stop?

4. Did you agree with Spike when he said, "They'll never get me on that engine again!" Why?

5. When did you know that there would not be a crash?

6. How did Dave think and act quickly to help avoid a dangerous situation?

Prewrite

Pretend that Dave and Spike have grown older and have returned to visit Old 88 with a group of children. What would you ask Dave and Spike about the way they feel about coming back to visit Old 88? What would you ask them about how the retired engine looks?

Draft

Make a list of questions that the children might ask Dave and Spike in an interview. Then answer those questions as you think Dave and Spike might have answered them. When you have done this, change papers with a classmate and answer your classmate's questions. Give each other suggestions about how to make the questions more interesting.

Revise

If necessary, change your questions to make the interview more interesting.

How have the changes in the steam-engine locomotive played an important part in improving transportation?

Steam-engine Trains

by Peter Roop

The Race of the *Tom Thumb*

The great race to Baltimore, Maryland, took place on a sunny fall day in 1830. Hundreds of people were there to watch. The tiny steam-engine locomotive, *Tom Thumb*, raced against a powerful, gray horse. Some people hoped the horse would win the race. Others wanted *Tom Thumb*, the "iron horse," to win.

The starting signal was given. Peter Cooper, the man who built *Tom Thumb,* opened a valve on his tiny steam engine. The iron wheels slowly began turning. The passengers aboard the train cheered as *Tom Thumb* puffed down the tracks.

The strong horse first trotted, then broke into a gallop. The passengers in the cart behind the horse shouted happily as they pulled ahead of the steam engine. The horse was soon in the lead.

Peter Cooper opened the steam valve wider and threw some wood onto the engine's fire. *Tom Thumb* rolled faster and faster. The locomotive quickly caught up with the horse. The horse tried to run as hard as it could. Then *Tom Thumb,* passengers cheering loudly, passed the horse.

Suddenly something in the steam engine broke and *Tom Thumb* lost power. Because Peter Cooper couldn't repair the engine in time, the horse passed *Tom Thumb* and won the race. Even though *Tom Thumb* lost the race, many people began to think that steam-engine locomotives would soon be carrying people and goods across America.

The Steam Age

The first railroads were "roads of rails." During the 1700's, miners in England used these "roads of rails" to move heavy piles of rock. Early trains were carts pulled by horses over the rails. One man built an engine powered by steam to move the carts. His idea worked and the first steam-engine locomotive was invented. Soon people were being transported by steam-powered locomotives.

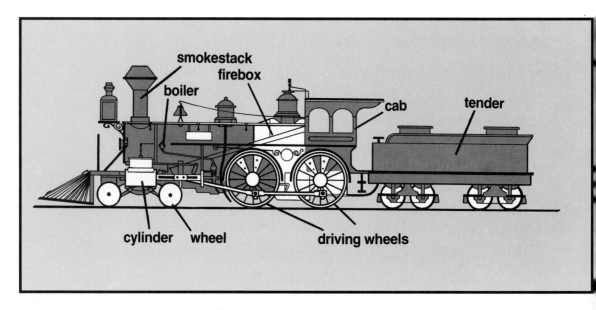

Early American Steam Engine

The first American steam engines burned wood to power the locomotive. The wood was burned in a firebox. The firebox heated water in the engine's boiler. The boiling water turned to steam. The steam pushed pistons inside the cylinders connected to the wheels. The wheels turned and the locomotive rolled down the track.

The engineer decided how much steam would turn the pistons. He could speed up or slow down the locomotive by opening or shutting valves. The fire-man kept a fire burning in the firebox.

Later, steam-engine locomotives burned coal. The coal was stored behind the engine in a car called a tender. The water, used to make steam, was also stored in the tender.

Steam-engine Improvements

Engineers and inventors worked to make steam-engine locomotives better, safer, and faster. The first engines sent sparks shooting high into the air causing many fires along the tracks. To control the sparks, a "balloon-shape" smokestack came into being. The top of this smokestack was wide enough to hold a screen that would catch the sparks.

As the engines became more powerful, they could pull more cars. Stopping a long train became very hard. Each car had its own brake. In order to stop the train, the engineer made the wheels spin back-wards. The brakeman ran along a "catwalk" on top of the cars. He hopped from car to car turning the brake handles.

In 1868 George Westinghouse invented a better way of stopping trains. His idea was to use air pressure on the wheels to make them stop. All of the brakes on cars were joined together. The engineer just had to pull one handle and every car would stop. Westinghouse's invention made train travel much safer. The old hand brakes were left on each car just in case of an emergency.

Safety Features

The earliest locomotives had no whistles. Often an engineer did not know if a train was coming in the other direction. This was very dangerous and there were many accidents.

In 1837 an engineer was working with a valve. When some steam was accidentally let out, it made a loud noise. The train whistle was born. Soon engineers could pull a cord to signal the crew or to let people know a train was coming.

Different whistle sounds had different meanings. One long whistle signaled that the train was coming into a station. A short whistle told the crew to stop the train. There was also a whistle for backing off the main track onto a small side track called a siding. Since there was only one set of tracks, one train had to wait on the siding while another train passed on the main track.

The telegraph, invented in 1844, became an important tool for the railroads. Telegraph messages could be sent from station to station. To receive a telegraph message, an engineer slowed down the train at the station. The station agent either threw the message to the fireman, or the agent handed the message to him on a long pole. When an engineer wanted to send a message, he could leave one with the station agent. Then the agent would telegraph the message to an agent at the other station and the message would be passed to another train in the same way.

From the days of the earliest steam-engine locomotives, like *Tom Thumb*, trains have played an important part in America. Trains have moved people and goods quickly and safely across the country. They have been responsible for the fast settling of the western part of the United States. They have brought adventure and excitement to thousands of railroad people and travelers alike.

1. How have the changes in the steam-engine locomotive played an important part in improving transportation?

2. Why was the race of the *Tom Thumb* an important event in the history of the steam engine?

3. What do you think was the most important invention connected with the steam-engine locomotive?

4. Why was the invention of the whistle important?

5. How did you know that air brakes might not work every time they were needed?

6. How have steam-engine trains played an important part in transportation?

Prewrite

This story gives us a lot of information and facts about trains. Look back over the story and think about some of the new information you learned. Think about what it would have been like to be a young helper on an early steam-engine trip. Think about what it would have been like to watch the race of the *Tom Thumb*. Discuss some of your ideas with a classmate.

Draft

Choose one of the activities below:

1. Pretend that you are a young helper on an early steam-engine journey. On your adventurous trip, you are along to help out the engineer and the fireman. Write to your family about all that you are doing.

2. Imagine that you witnessed the race between *Tom Thumb* and the horse-drawn cart, and that you are a newscaster. Write a report that might be read on the radio about the race.

Revise

Exchange stories with a classmate. Write a list of questions that you have about his or her story. Look over the questions about your story. Think about the questions and make necessary changes and improvements in your story.

Trains at Night

by Frances M. Frost

I like the whistle of trains at night,
The fast trains thundering by so proud!
They rush and rumble across the world,
They ring wild bells and they toot so loud!

But I love better the slower trains.
They take their time through the world instead,
And whistle softly and stop to tuck
Each sleepy blinking town in bed!

Characterization

An author uses several ways to help you understand characters in stories. Read the paragraph
below to see one way this is done.

Dave was an engineer and a good
thinker. When the brakes did not work on
his train, he acted fast. Dave threw a message to the station agent on the platform
telling him to keep the other train on the
siding. Dave's fast thinking prevented a
crash.

In this paragraph, you learned that Dave was a
fast thinker. The author gave you this information.
Now read the next paragraph to discover a second
way in which an author might help you understand
the same character.

"I have to do something right away,"
Dave thought as he tried the brakes
again. "Maybe if I get a note to the station
in Cantwell, they can send a message to
hold No. 64 at Parkersville."

In this paragraph, what does the author do? The author helps you to know what Dave is like by sharing Dave's thoughts, words, and actions with you.

Now read to discover a third way an author might use to help you understand Dave.

The station agent shook his head as he told how Dave got the message to him.

"He held it up as the train came near, so I could see it. Then he threw it hard toward the station. I sent the message to Parkersville just in time."

"It's a good thing that Dave could think that fast," said another station worker.

How does the author help you to get to know Dave in these paragraphs? You understand Dave by reading what other characters in the story say about him.

As you read, remember that an author may help you to understand a character by:
- describing the character;
- telling what the character thinks, says, and does;
- using other characters to tell about a character.

Tall tales about John Henry have been told for many years. Why is John Henry remembered?

John Henry

by Anne Maley

In the 1870's, a man named John Henry came from Tennessee to work as a steel driver for the Chesapeake and Ohio Railroad in West Virginia. John Henry helped to build the Big Bend Tunnel through the West Virginia mountains. He died building that tunnel, after proving that a machine could not beat him at driving steel.

Ever since then, people have made up songs and stories, or tall tales, about John Henry, the steel-driving man. Through these songs and tales, people remember John Henry as a strong, brave man who had the spirit to say "I can do it" and who always did his best. This is one way that the story of John Henry is told.

Soon after John Henry was born, he reached out for his daddy's hammer hanging on the wall.

John Henry's father looked proudly at his son. "That boy is going to be a steel-driving man," he said. "I know it as surely as I know that rivers run to the sea."

John Henry was a few weeks old when he picked up his daddy's five-pound hammer and swung it in the air. Whoosh! Whoosh! Whoosh!

John Henry was only two months old when he began using the hammer to hit rocks in the yard. Bang! Bang! Bang! Then he told his mama, "I was born with a hammer in my hand. I was born to be a steel-driving man."

As a young man, John Henry was eight feet tall and had arms as big as tree trunks. He helped his mama around the house and his daddy on the farm. He could work harder and play harder than anyone around. It was not long before he began to think about going out into the world on his own.

Often John Henry would lie in bed at night and listen to the long, lonely sounds of the trains going by. He dreamed about working on a railroad somewhere, using a big hammer to drive steel.

One night John Henry told his mama and daddy about a dream he had. "I was working on the railroad," John Henry said. "I was swinging my mighty hammer and driving steel right into the ground. When I swung it in the air, a rainbow circled around my shoulder. When my hammer hit the spike, sparks flew into the sky."

The next morning, John Henry said good-bye to his mama and daddy. Then he left to find his own way in the world. He knew he could do any work and do it well. He just had to find the right job for him.

John Henry found his first work on farms and in cotton fields. He became the best cotton picker in the South. He could pick three bales of cotton a day, more than any other worker. He wanted work that paid better, so he found a job on a riverboat that traveled the river carrying goods from place to place. Yet all the while he was thinking about that hammer and waiting for his time to come.

While working on the riverboat, John Henry heard that the Chesapeake and Ohio Railroad needed workers. They wanted strong men who could help build the Big Bend Tunnel through the mountains in West Virginia. John Henry left his job on the riverboat and headed for West Virginia.

On the way there he met a girl named Polly Ann. She was the prettiest girl he had ever seen. Soon he and Polly Ann were married, and they set off to West Virginia. As they were walking through the mountains, John Henry heard a sweet sound. "Listen, Polly Ann," he said. "It's the sound of hammers striking steel!" So they followed the sounds until there it was — the C & O Railroad! The railroad tracks ran right up to the foot of a huge, rocky mountain and then stopped.

John Henry watched the men work. He watched a man called a *shaker* hold a steel spike in place on the rock. He watched another man swing his ten-pound hammer in the air and whomp the steel into the stone. Again and again, the steel driver drove the steel deeper into the rock. When the hole was deep enough, another man put explosives in the hole to blow the rock away. Little by little, the tunnel would be blown out of the mountain.

John Henry walked over to the boss, Captain Tommy, and said, "I'm John Henry, a steel-driving man, and I'm looking for a job."

"You're big, but what do you know about driving steel?" asked Captain Tommy.

"I'm a natural man," answered John Henry. "Driving steel is just a natural thing for me to do."

"Then take this twenty-pound hammer," said Captain Tommy. "We'll see what a natural man can do. I'll even give you my best steel shaker, Little Will, to hold the spike."

As Little Will held the spike, John Henry swung the twenty-pound hammer high over his head. Then he brought the hammer down and it landed in the middle of the spike, sending the spike halfway into the rock. John Henry swung again, and this time the spike went all the way into the rock.

Neither Little Will nor Captain Tommy could believe their eyes. "I've never seen a man drive a spike so far in two blows," said Captain Tommy. "John Henry, you're hired!"

After that, Little Will and John Henry worked together every day. John Henry swung his mighty hammer, and Little Will held the spikes. John Henry sang as he worked, and Little Will sang along:

There ain't no hammer upon this mountain
Rings like mine, boys, rings like mine.
This old hammer rings like silver,
Shines like gold, boys, shines like gold.

After a while, John Henry began swinging two twenty-pound hammers, one in each hand. People came from miles around to watch him work and hear him sing.

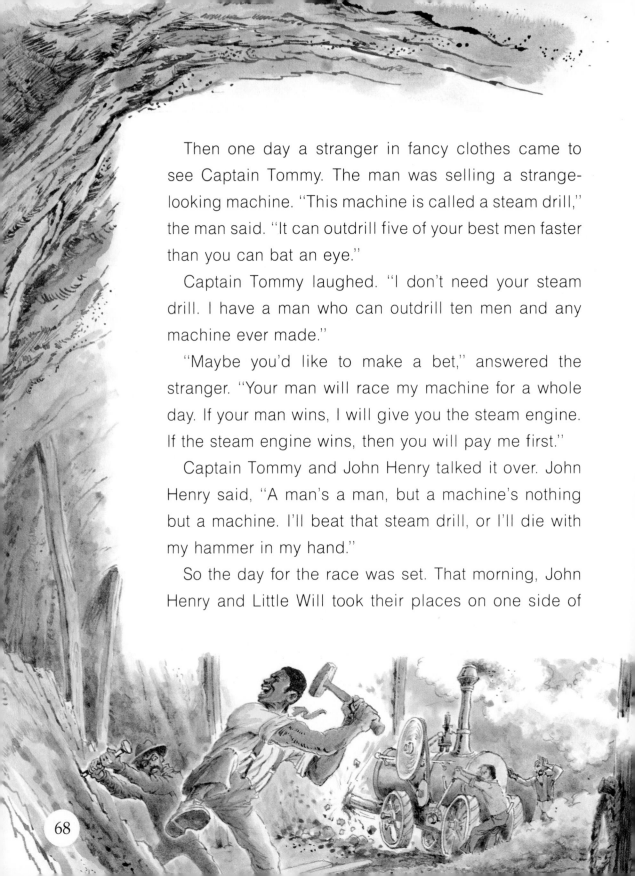

Then one day a stranger in fancy clothes came to see Captain Tommy. The man was selling a strange-looking machine. "This machine is called a steam drill," the man said. "It can outdrill five of your best men faster than you can bat an eye."

Captain Tommy laughed. "I don't need your steam drill. I have a man who can outdrill ten men and any machine ever made."

"Maybe you'd like to make a bet," answered the stranger. "Your man will race my machine for a whole day. If your man wins, I will give you the steam engine. If the steam engine wins, then you will pay me first."

Captain Tommy and John Henry talked it over. John Henry said, "A man's a man, but a machine's nothing but a machine. I'll beat that steam drill, or I'll die with my hammer in my hand."

So the day for the race was set. That morning, John Henry and Little Will took their places on one side of the tunnel. The steam drill was on the other side. Polly Ann joined the crowd who had gathered around the tunnel to watch. When the judge blew his whistle, the race began. Soon the tunnel walls shook with the chug and clatter of the steam drill and the whoosh and clang of John Henry's hammer striking steel.

The race went on and on in the hot, dark tunnel. The whole mountain rang with the chug and clatter and clang of man and machine driving steel. Only once did the machine break down and need to have a worn part replaced. Only once did John Henry stop to get water.

Just when it seemed that the noise and the drilling would never end, the judge blew the whistle. The race was over.

The judge examined the drilling holes and declared, "John Henry drilled the most holes and the deepest holes. He has beaten the machine!" The people clapped and cheered.

Polly Ann ran to John Henry and found him lying on the ground with a hammer in his hand. The doctor who examined him said, "His heart just stopped. John Henry, the natural steel-driving man, died with a hammer in his hand."

1. Why do people remember John Henry?

2. What happened when John Henry raced the steam drill?

3. Why did John Henry want a job with the railroad?

4. Who do you think really won the contest? Why?

5. What do you think John Henry meant when he said, "I'm a natural man"?

6. John Henry was able to do some things better than other people because of his "I can do it" spirit. What were some things John Henry could do?

Think and Write

Prewrite

The author of "John Henry" wrote some unbelievable things about him. These things help to make the story a tall tale. Tall tales also need some believable things in them. Think about someone who could be the main character in a tall tale. What real things that describe the character would you include in the tall tale? What unbelievable things could you write about the character?

Draft

Write a tall tale about the person you selected. Be sure to include enough information to make it seem real, and enough unbelievable things to make it a tall tale.

Revise

Read your tall tale to a classmate, and then listen to your classmate's story. Does the main character of the tall tale seem real? Are there enough unbelievable details to make it a tall tale? Talk to your classmate about how his or her story might be improved. Change papers and do the same thing with your paper. Then change your story to make it better.

Thinking About "Passports"

The characters in this unit carried different kinds of passports. The boots the shoemaker made of very fine leather were his passport to see the king. He also needed to be wise and clever to get past the guards.

You also read about passports that helped people learn, grow, and change. Marco Polo discovered a different way of life when he traveled to China. Remember how Molly learned to be proud of her background? What did Dave learn about himself when he was faced with a dangerous situation?

John Henry was a very unusual character. How did the author of the story help you get to know John Henry? What passport did John Henry use to grow and change?

As you read other stories, look for the ways you learn about the characters. Watch to see how their adventures change them. Look for the passports they use to grow as people.

1. How are the adventures of the shoemaker and those of Marco Polo alike? How are they different?

2. How did Molly and John Henry change? How did the change help each character grow?

3. What were some problems that each major character in a fiction selection in this unit had to solve?

4. How are Dave's situation and John Henry's situation alike? What did both characters have to do in order to solve a problem?

5. Marco Polo and Molly faced situations that helped them learn about new ideas. How were their situations alike? How were they different?

Unit 2

Portholes

A porthole is a round window or opening in the side of a ship. If two people look through the same porthole, they may see different things or they may see the same thing differently.

Sometimes people change their minds about what they see. Have you ever read a story and noticed how the character's view of a situation or problem changed by the end of the story?

When you read the stories in this unit, pretend you are looking at the characters through a porthole. Watch closely. Does the way they see things change? What do they do because of the changes? You may want to ask yourself what you would do if the same things happened to you.

The Hundred Dresses *by Eleanor Estes. Harcourt Brace Jovanovich.* When Wanda tells the children about her hundred dresses and many other clothes, they tease her. Maddie feels sorry for Wanda but goes along with the teasing anyway. Later in the story, Maddie learns much about Wanda, herself, and her friends.

Kermit the Hermit *by Bill Peet. Houghton.* Kermit the crab lives alone and does not want any friends. When a boy saves his life, Kermit changes his ways.

A New True Book: Animals of the Sea and Shore *by Illa Podendorf. Childrens Press.* This book is about the many different creatures that live in the sea and on the seashore.

Grandaddy's Place *by Helen V. Griffith. Greenwillow.* Janetta doesn't like Grandaddy's run-down place in the country until she sees things the way Grandaddy sees them.

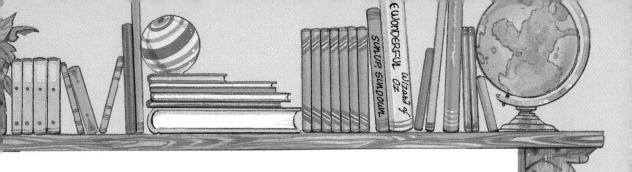

Night of Ghosts and Hermits *by Mary Stolz. Harcourt Brace Jovanovich.* Claudell's brothers just play on the beach, but he is interested in marine life. You will be surprised at the creatures that live at the edge of the sea.

Gloomy Louie *by Phyllis Green. Whitman.* Louie always worries that he won't do well and will disappoint his family. When he saves a neighbor from a fire, he realizes that each of us is important.

Discovering the Stars *by Laurence Santrey. Troll.* This book describes the constellations and different kinds of stars. It also tells about how the stars were used in the past and how they are used today.

The Wonderful Flight to the Mushroom Planet *by Eleanor Cameron. Little.* Mr. Bass wants David and Chuck to get the spaceship they built ready and set off to a secret planet called Basidium. Can they do it?

Miss Moody likes to walk on the beach after a storm. What does she find on the beach that could cause her a problem? How does she solve the problem?

Do Not Open

story and pictures by Brinton Turkle

Miss Moody lived at land's end with Captain Kidd. Captain Kidd wasn't the famous pirate; he was a cat. One morning after a storm, Miss Moody found him washed up on the beach. He was nearly drowned. She took care of him until he was well, and he repaid her kindness by keeping her cottage free of mice.

Captain Kidd hated storms. Miss Moody loved them. Just about everything in her cottage had been found on the beach after a storm, even the handsome banjo clock over her fireplace. The only thing wrong with the clock was that it wouldn't go. The hands always pointed to twenty minutes to four o'clock.

Late one September afternoon, the sky grew dark. A strong wind started to blow. Miss Moody knew what was coming. She shut the windows and lit a cheery fire in the fireplace. Captain Kidd wouldn't come out from under the bed.

Lightning flashed. Thunder crashed. Rain dashed against the windows.

Was Miss Moody worried? Not a bit. Her sturdy house had been built by a sea captain. It could ride out any storm. She smiled as she wondered what surprises might be on the beach in the morning.

After a quick breakfast the next morning, Miss Moody got out the old wheelbarrow. She and Captain Kidd were ready for the treasure hunt.

The first thing she found was a pretty tin box which was just what she needed for her postcard collection. She stowed the box in her wheelbarrow.

Then she saw something red in the sand. It was a rug with one corner missing, but it would look just lovely in her bedroom. The torn end could be tucked under a chest, so she stowed the rug in her wheelbarrow.

She next came upon a pile of driftwood. What beautiful colors it would make burning in her fireplace! There was too much for one load, so she stowed as much as she could in her wheelbarrow and headed home. She would come back for the rest later.

Captain Kidd was the first to see the deep purple bottle and he didn't like it at all. It was closed tight and these words were scratched on it: *Do Not Open.*

As Miss Moody picked up the bottle, a voice said, "What do you want more than anything in the world?"

More than anything in the world, Miss Moody wanted her banjo clock to run: to tick and bong like banjo clocks are supposed to do. She was certainly not about to tell this to a stranger. "None of your beeswax!" she snapped and turned around to see who had sneaked up behind her.

No one was anywhere in sight. She couldn't even see Captain Kidd for a moment, and then she noticed his tail twitching from under the wheelbarrow.

"I'll give you whatever you want if you'll just let me out, please."

The voice was coming from the bottle! Miss Moody almost dropped it. "Who are you?" she demanded.

"I'm a poor little child. I was put in here by a wicked person and now I want to go home to my mama. Pull out the stopper and please free me!"

Should she open the bottle? Miss Moody could not stand hearing a child cry. She tugged at the stopper, and suddenly the stopper popped out.

Smoke started to trickle out of the bottle, so Miss Moody threw the bottle on the sand. The smoke came out in billows, twisting into a big black cloud, and then the bottle broke. From inside the cloud came terrible laughter. It was not the laughter of a child.

"Free!" roared a voice like thunder.

The smoke cleared away and Miss Moody was staring at the biggest, ugliest creature she had ever seen.

"Thank you, madam," it said. "Too bad you didn't make a wish. You could have had anything you wanted—gold, gems, a palace. I could have made you a queen or a president."

"You are just a bad, bad dream," Miss Moody said.

"Why aren't you afraid of me?" the creature asked.

"Because I'm not afraid of anything I don't believe in, and I don't believe in you for a minute."

The creature grew bigger and uglier. "Now are you afraid of me?" it demanded.

"No," said Miss Moody.

The creature grew even bigger and even uglier. "Are you still not afraid of me?" it growled.

"Getting bigger and uglier doesn't scare me," said Miss Moody. "I'm only afraid of mice, and you can't grow small like a little mouse."

The creature disappeared. At Miss Moody's feet was a tiny gray mouse.

Captain Kidd jumped so quickly the mouse didn't have time to squeak. He swallowed it.

"Captain!" cried Miss Moody. "Are you all right?"

Captain Kidd stretched. Miss Moody, Captain Kidd, and the wheelbarrow all went home, shaking a little bit.

Before they got to the cottage, Miss Moody heard it: "Bong! bong! bong! bong! bong! bong! bong! bong!" She rushed inside.

The handsome banjo clock over the fireplace was ticking away busily. The hands pointed to one minute past eight o'clock.

1. How was Miss Moody's trip to the beach after this storm different from her other trips?

2. How did Miss Moody solve her problem at the beach?

3. There was another surprise waiting for Miss Moody when she got home. What was it?

4. How do you think Miss Moody felt when she got home?

5. When did you know the creature wouldn't hurt Miss Moody?

6. Miss Moody showed courage. How did this help her overcome her problem?

**Think
and
Write**

Prewrite

Miss Moody was a beachcomber who liked to search along the shore for useful items. Think about what it would be like to walk down a deserted, quiet beach. Think about some of the things you might find or that you would like to find, and how you might use them. Make a list of the items.

Draft

Choose one of the activities below:

1. Imagine that you have just taken a long walk along a shore and that you, like Miss Moody, are a beachcomber. Write a story about your walk and the things you found. Be sure to include how they will be useful to you and why you want to keep them. Remember to use your list.

2. Pretend that you are a beachcomber, like Miss Moody, and that you have found one very interesting thing. Write a story about what you have found. Weave your story around this one interesting item.

Revise

Read your story over again to yourself. Does it seem connected? Try to use words and phrases that will make your story stick together better. Make any changes that will help your story to be more connected.

National Council of Teachers of English
Award Poet

Until I Saw the Sea

by Lilian Moore

Until I saw the sea
I did not know
that wind
could wrinkle water so.

I never knew
that sun
could splinter a whole sea of blue.

Nor
did I know before,
a sea breathes in and out
upon a shore.

Children's Choices Author

A treasure hunt on the beach is a way for Elisabeth and Charles to learn about things that live there. What are some of the things that Elisabeth and Charles learn?

Elisabeth, the Treasure Hunter

(adapted from a story)
by Felice Holman

Elisabeth's mother packed a "treasure" in a tin box so Elisabeth could be a treasure hunter. Elisabeth's father was going to bury the treasure on the beach and give Elisabeth some clues to help her find it. When Elisabeth and her father got to the beach, they met Professor Eckleberry and his grandson, Charles. They asked the professor to bury the treasure for them and give them some clues. Charles decided that he wanted to help Elisabeth and her father find the treasure.

"Let's take a look at the clue," Papa said.

Three rocks near one rock,
Masqueraders dwell.
From house to house,
From shell to shell.

"That means we will find something or other, in or near something, that is near three rocks, that are near one rock," said Papa.

They walked along, and then Elisabeth called, "Here are three big rocks at the edge of the water!"

Then Charles said, "There's one rock all by itself farther up on the shore."

Elisabeth and Charles ran down to the edge of the water. The rocks stood like mountains around a small pool of water.

"It's full of snails," said Elisabeth, "and they're walking around pretty fast."

Papa came up to the pool. "If they're walking around pretty fast, you'd better look at them again. The snails I know are very slow-moving."

"They have awfully long legs," Charles said.

"What you have found is a hermit crab," said Papa leaning over the pool. "His shell once belonged to a snail. He has no shell of his own so he borrows one from a snail and uses it for a house."

"That's the clue!" cried Charles.

Papa whipped the paper out of his pocket. He read: " 'Three rocks near one rock.' Well, that's right, anyway. 'Masqueraders dwell?' "

"That's the hermit crab!" cried Elisabeth. "He's borrowed a snail's shell. Hey, look at that! There's a piece of paper in the pool, partly hidden under a shell."

Charles reached into the pool for the paper. Papa took the wet piece of paper from Charles.

Papa frowned. "It says:"

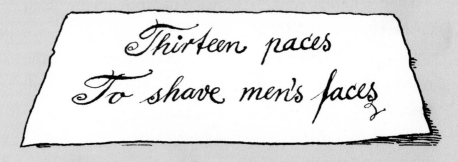

Thirteen paces
To shave men's faces

"It does say 'thirteen paces.' Let's walk and count our steps," Papa said.

Charles took the biggest steps he could, and counted thirteen paces. Elisabeth didn't get as far. Papa's paces took him farthest of all because his legs were the longest.

"All right now," Papa called, "let's look around and see what will shave men's faces."

They formed their line again and walked along, heads down, looking closely at the wet sand.

"Tide's coming in," Papa said. "We'll have to hurry. Charles, your grandfather said the clues were only good for an hour."

"Look at this funny, sharp shell sticking out of the sand," said Charles.

"Here's another," declared Elisabeth.

"These clams are called razor clams. See, this empty shell is shaped like an old-fashioned razor," said Papa.

"Razors!" exclaimed Elisabeth.

"Exactly," said Papa. " 'Thirteen paces to shave men's faces.' Look! I was just turning over this razor-clam shell, and there on the shell . . . do you see what I see?"

"It's another clue!" cried Elisabeth.

Papa looked closely at the shell, and read:

Little feathers lead the way
To beads of white on rocks of gray

Charles started walking in a way that reminded Elisabeth of a tightrope walker in the circus, putting one foot in front of the other and balancing with his arms.

"What are you doing?" she asked.

"I'm following the footsteps," he declared. Elisabeth looked down and saw some faint tracks in the sand.

"A gull has made those faint tracks," said Papa.

"They're very feathery footprints," declared Elisabeth.

"Feathery!" exclaimed Charles. *"Feathers!"*

" 'Little *feathers* lead the way . . .' " said Elisabeth. "Let's follow the gull tracks!"

The gull tracks led down the shore and to the stone jetty. Charles and Elisabeth climbed up onto the nearest of the large rocks.

"Look!" Charles called. "The jetty is covered with thousands of little white cabbages. Ow! They're sharp!"

"They look like beads to me," said Elisabeth.

"What kind of beads?" asked Papa.

"White beads," said Elisabeth.

" 'Beads of white,' " Papa said.

" 'Rocks of gray,' " Charles added.

"The clue!" cried Elisabeth.

"What are beads doing here on the rock?" asked Charles.

"Well," Papa said, "although these look like beads, they are really a small animal called a barnacle. Many of them are closed up tightly over a little, upside-down animal that is waiting for the sea to come back."

"There are barnacles on this rope, too," Charles declared, tugging on a rope he found in the water.

"Papa!" cried Elisabeth. "Charles! It's our tin box! It's the treasure tied to the end of this rope!"

"Maybe the tide came up over it," said Charles.

"Here, let me help," Papa said.

Inside the box everything was dry as could be, and there was the treasure, looking very good. There were large chunks of gold, looking like beautiful peaches; pieces of jade, looking like bunches of grapes shining in the sun; and beautiful gems, looking like red, yellow, and green apples.

"The tide is coming in quickly, now. We'd better be moving off the rocks," Papa said. He led them down onto the sand.

"If we eat the treasure we found, we will have no treasure left," said Elisabeth.

Elisabeth looked at the beach and down at her feet where the water was running onto the shore. She saw the little creatures the tide was bringing in and leaving on the beach.

"Do you know what?" Elisabeth said. "The beach is a kind of treasure, isn't it?"

1. How do Elisabeth and Charles learn about the things that live on the beach?

2. What does Elisabeth discover about the beach?

3. What do Elisabeth, Papa, and Charles do once they find their treasure?

4. What do you think about the clues?

5. When did you know that the treasure hunt would be more fun than Elisabeth's mother had planned?

6. What does the author want her readers to learn?

Prewrite

Think about the clever clues the Professor wrote for Elisabeth and Charles. Think about a place where you might hide a treasure. Now, think about clues or messages that you might write to lead someone to the treasure. Copy and complete the following chart to help you organize your ideas.

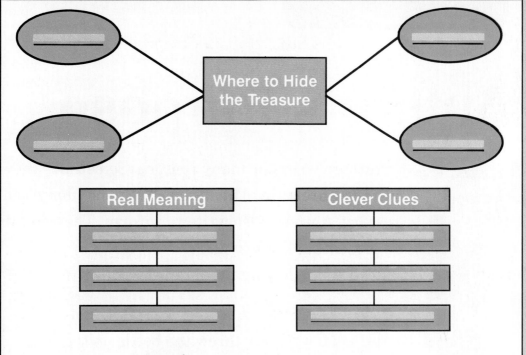

Where to Hide
the Treasure

Real Meaning

Clever Clues

Draft

Use the information from your chart to write a paragraph about your treasure hunt. Write at least three clues that will lead a friend to the treasure. Try to make your clues interesting.

Revise

Share your clues with a classmate. Explain what they mean. Looking at each other's clues, discuss how you might make them clearer or more interesting. Make changes to improve your clues.

Author's Purpose

Authors write for many reasons. Sometimes they write to **entertain.** Their stories may be funny, sad, or scary. Authors also write to **inform.** They do this by presenting facts or ideas.

Read the following paragraph.

Smoke started to trickle out of the bottle, so Miss Moody threw the bottle on the sand. The smoke came out in billows, twisting into a big black cloud, and then the bottle broke. From inside the cloud came terrible laughter. It was not the laughter of a child.

What was the author's purpose? The author's purpose was to entertain you.

Read the next paragraph and think about the authors' purpose as you read.

98

There are many different kinds of shells. They can be round like the moon, long like a jackknife, or shaped like boxes, fans, or tops. The shells we find are usually empty, but once there were soft bodies inside.

from *A First Look at Seashells*
by Millicent E. Selsam and Joyce Hunt

What was the authors' purpose? Why do you think so? The authors' purpose was to inform by sharing facts and information about seashells with you.

Now decide the authors' purpose in each of the following paragraphs.

A

Most kites have three main parts. The frame is made of wood or plastic sticks. Paper or material is used for the cover. String is then wrapped around the stick and used for a flying line.

B

The audience roared with laughter. The little clown followed the big clown's steps. He pantomimed what the big clown did. The big clown didn't know he was being followed.

What were the authors' purposes for writing paragraphs **A** and **B**? Paragraph **A** was written to inform. Paragraph **B** is a story written to entertain.

As you read a selection, think about why the author wrote it. Ask yourself if the author's purpose was to inform or to entertain.

A beach is alive with many living things. Read to see how a hermit crab finds a new home.

A Hermit Hunts a New Home

by Peter and Connie Roop

Night had come to the seashore and the bright moon rose over the ocean. The tide was out now and the water had moved to a low level, leaving behind many living and nonliving things.

Seaweed lay where the high tide had left it. Empty shells of clams and snails were scattered on the sand. Wet rocks poked up like small islands from the sand. Driftwood lay on the beach.

Whoosh! A wave crashed onto the shore. The foaming water rushed up the beach, carrying a hermit crab with it. The wave dropped the crab onto the sand.

The hermit crab stretched out its legs and claws and quickly dug its legs into the sand. Another wave washed over it. When the wave left, the crab ran up the beach out of the reach of the next wave. It knew the tide was rising. The hermit crab did not want to return to the ocean yet. It was looking for a bigger shell. The moon snail shell that the hermit crab lived in was too small. Like all hermit crabs, it changed shells as it grew. It would search the shore for a shell that was its size.

Suddenly, a night heron walked down the beach. The crab did not move for a long time. A hermit crab would make a good meal for the hungry heron. The heron saw the crab and began moving toward it. The crab ran to safety in a pile of seaweed.

Silently, the heron moved closer and poked the seaweed looking for the hermit crab. The hermit crab stayed hidden in the seaweed until the heron finally flew away. When it was clear, the crab was able to continue looking for a new home.

The hermit crab saw a large whelk shell. The crab turned the shell over with its claws. Then it looked into the shell. The hermit crab felt inside with its claws and decided to try the shell on for size.

Carefully, the hermit crab crawled out of its own shell. For only a few minutes its soft lobster-like body was unprotected. The hermit crab quickly pushed itself into the whelk shell.

The hermit crab moved as far as it could into the shell, but parts of its soft body stuck out. The shell was too small. The hermit crab quickly backed out of the whelk and returned to its own moon shell. The crab continued its search.

The hermit dragged its shell over some small clam holes. Bothered by the crab, the clams squirted small jets of water up into the air. The crab moved on.

The hermit crab found a razor

clam shell. The clam had been broken and eaten by a gull. The hermit crab could never fit into this kind of shell because it is too long and narrow. So the hermit crab moved on, dragging its shell behind it.

The bright moon shone on the beach. Every few moments the crab stopped walking and looked for enemies. The night heron had not returned. Far ahead, the crab saw some rocks and it moved slowly toward them.

On the way to the rocks, the crab stopped to eat some tiny fish that had washed up on the beach. The moon was high in the sky when the crab reached the rocks. The hermit crab walked around the pile of rocks. It did not find any other shells so it began climbing the rocks.

The rocks were covered with long strands of seaweed. Several young green crabs were hiding under the seaweed. As the hermit crab got near, the little crabs moved out of the hermit crab's way. The little crabs did not want to become dinner for the hermit crab.

The hermit crab stopped when it reached the top of the rocks. The rocks formed a bowl-shaped circle. A pool of water was trapped inside the bowl. This water, or tide pool, had been left by the last high tide. The hermit crab thought it might find a new shell there.

The crab climbed over a ring of white barnacles around the tide pool. The tiny, sharp barnacles closed their shells as the crab went by. When it had passed, the barnacles opened their shells again to catch food.

The hermit crab watched a smaller hermit crab crawling across the tide pool. The hermit crab did not know it but this hermit crab was also looking for an empty shell in which to live.

The hermit crab saw a sea star at the bottom of the tide pool. The crab walked towards the star. The sea star was wrapped around a blue mussel shell, using its five strong arms to open the mussel shell. When it opened the shell, the sea star would eat the mussel inside.

Dozens of snails moved slowly over the rocky bottom of the tide pool. The snails were eating tiny plants growing on the rocks. They grazed like a herd of small, round cows. The hermit crawled past the snails. None of the snail shells would be large enough.

Finally, the hermit crab discovered a large, white whelk shell. It touched the shell and found the shell was empty. Next, the hermit crab reached inside the shell with its claws and felt back as far as it could. The shell seemed to be the right size.

The hermit crab crawled out of its own shell and backed into the whelk shell. The crab pushed itself as far as it could into the shell. The whelk shell fit nicely. The crab had found a new home.

The hermit crab had searched hard for a new shell and now it was very hungry. So the hermit crab began to look for food. It left its empty moon snail shell behind.

Waves were splashing over the rocks into the tide pool now. The tide was high. The hermit crab pulled its claws over the opening of its new shell, closing it like a door. A wave picked the hermit crab up and rolled it into the ocean. Back on the bottom of the ocean, the crab uncurled its claws and began looking for more food.

In the tide pool the other hermit crab found the empty moon snail shell. It felt inside the empty shell. This hermit crab turned the shell around with its claws. Quickly it moved into a new home and left its empty shell for another hermit crab.

1. What are some of the living and nonliving things that can be found on a beach?

2. How does a hermit crab find a new home?

3. What might happen on a beach during low tide?

4. How did you feel when the heron was looking for the hermit crab?

5. What did you read that made you think the hermit crab would find a new home?

6. Why is low tide an active time at the beach?

Prewrite

The story tells what a day in the life of a hermit crab would be like. Take some time to observe an animal. It could be a pet at home, a classroom pet, or a squirrel in a nearby park. Think about what this animal's life is like. What does it do all day? How could you write a story about the animal you selected without telling its name?

Draft

Write a story that tells about what a specific animal does in a day. Describe as many things as you can think of that the animal does as it goes through a day. Be sure to give the reader a good feeling for what the animal's life is like. Remember, don't use the name of the animal (dog, cat) in the story.

Revise

Read your story to your classmates without letting them know what animal you wrote about. See if they can guess the animal. If they cannot, what details could you add to help them guess? Make the necessary changes in your story so that it clearly tells what the animal's life is like.

Reference Source: Dictionary

A dictionary is a useful tool for finding the definition, or meaning, of a word. A dictionary can also help you spell words and tell you how to pronounce them. A dictionary, just like an encyclopedia, is arranged in alphabetical order.

Three important parts of a dictionary page are the entry words, the guide words, and the pronunciation key.

---

giant   giraffe

gi·ant [jī′ənt] **1** *n.* An imaginary being in human form but a great deal larger and more powerful than a real person. **2** *n.* Any person, animal, or thing of great size, strength, intelligence or ability. **3** *adj.* Huge or great.

gib·bon [gib′ən] *n.* A slender, long-armed ape of SE Asia and the East Indies, that lives in trees.

gift [gift] *n.* **1** Something that is given; present. **2** A natural ability; talent: a *gift* for music.

gig·gle [gig′əl] *v.* **gig·gled, gig·gling,** *n.* **1** *v.* To laugh in a silly or nervous manner with high fluttering sounds. **2** *n.* Such a laugh. —**gig′ gler** *n.*

Gi·la monster [hē′lə] A large, poisonous lizard of the SW U.S. and northern Mexico. It is covered with black and orange scales.

■

gin·ger·snap [jin′jər·snap′] *n.* A small, flat, brittle cookie flavored with ginger and molasses.

ging·ham [ging′əm] *n.* A cotton fabric woven in solid colors, stripes, checks, or plaids.
Gingham goes back to a Malay word meaning *striped.*

gi·raffe [jə·raf′] *n.* An African animal that chews its cud. The tallest of all animals living today, it has a very long neck, long slender legs, and a spotted skin.

a	add	i	it	o͝o	took	oi	oil
ā	ace	ī	ice	o͞o	pool	ou	pout
â	care	o	odd	u	up	ng	ring
ä	palm	ō	open	û	burn	th	thin
e	end	ô	order	yo͞o	fuse	t͟h	this
ē	equal					zh	vision

ə = { a in *above*   e in *sicken*   i in *possible*
      { o in *melon*   u in *circus*

Gila monster

108

Entry Words

Find the words *giant, gift,* and *giggle* on the sample dictionary page. These words are printed in boldface and are listed in alphabetical order on the page. These and all the other boldface words on the page are the **entry words.** When you use the dictionary, look for the entry words.

Guide Words

Look at the two words *giant* and *giraffe* printed in blue at the top of the dictionary page. These are the **guide words** for this page. They tell you that the first entry word on the page is *giant* and that the last entry word is *giraffe.* All the other entry words on the page are in alphabetical order between these two guide words. Guide words are a useful way of quickly finding entry words.

Pronunciation Key

Look at the entry word *giant.* Next to it in brackets [ ], *giant* is respelled with letters and symbols that help you pronounce the word. To understand the sounds these symbols stand for, you need to use the **pronunciation key.** A short form of the key is usually shown at the bottom of the dictionary page. The full pronunciation key is always found at the front of the book.

Using Guide Words and Entry Words

The guide words on the sample dictionary page are *giant* and *giraffe*. Suppose you want to find the following words in the dictionary. Which would be on the same page with the guide words *giant* and *giraffe*?

gill, give, get, ginger

The words *gill* and *ginger* would be on the page because the letters *gil* and *gin* come after the first three letters of the guide word *giant* and before the first three letters of the guide word *giraffe*. The word *get* would not be on the same page because *get* comes before *giant* in alphabetical order. The word *give* would not be on that page because *give* comes after *giraffe* in alphabetical order.

Guide words are an important part of a dictionary page. By using alphabetical order and the guide words, you will find entry words more quickly than if you read every entry word on the page.

Look at the entry word *flipper* on the next page. Notice that it is printed in boldface type. Notice the numerals *1* and *2* in the definition for *flipper*. These numerals tell you that there are two meanings for the word. Which definition matches the way the word *flipper* is used in the sentence below the definition of *flipper*? Why?

> **flip·per** [flip′ər] *n.* **1** A broad, flat limb, as of a seal, adapted for swimming. **2** A broad, flat shoe like a fin, worn by skin divers.

The swimmer put on a mask and flippers before getting into the water.

The second definition fits the sentence because the meaning of the word *flipper* has to do with something a person puts on to help him or her swim.

Read the following entry words, definitions, and sentences. Decide which definition better fits the meaning if the word as it is used in the sentence.

> **dol·ly** [dol′ē] *n.* **1** A doll: a child's term. **2** A low, flat frame set on small wheels or rollers, used for moving heavy loads.

The band used the dolly to move the instruments.

> **sid·ing** [sī′ding] *n.* **1** A railroad track by the side of the main track, onto which cars may be switched. **2** A material, as overlapping boards, used to construct the outside walls of a house or building with a wooden frame.

After the siding on the house was painted, the house looked brand new.

Remember to use guide words to help you find a word quickly. Once you find the entry word, read all the definitions. Try each definition with the sentence in which the word appears. Then decide which definition best fits the word that is used in the sentence.

Jimmy and some other children are on a spaceship. What is Jimmy hoping to see as he looks at the screen?

In Space

by George Zebrowski

"What are we going to do?" Jimmy's brother asked. They were waiting for Jimmy to come up with a plan, or they would be left to drift in space forever.

Jimmy Wilson knew that his brother, Billy, and the six others were frightened. Suddenly he felt much older than any of them. They were all under ten. He was going to be thirteen. If he lived to see February 24, 2095, that is. Way down deep, Jimmy didn't feel all that much older than the others. It just seemed that way now, as he looked at their faces.

Turning away from Billy and the others, Jimmy remembered all that had happened. He thought of the wonderful summer he had spent on Lea, the Earth-like planet. Then he remembered how he had gotten on the large space liner and had taken off on the return flight to Earth. Jimmy had been on the ship's deck when everything began. The captain had told them that the ship's engines were out of control and could not be fixed. The engines would explode before they reached Earth.

Next, Jimmy thought about how one of the ship's officers had directed him, Billy, and the others onto the liner's lifeboat. Before the officer could get on himself, the metal door had closed. Then the engines of the lifeboat had started, and it had pulled away from the liner. Jimmy and the others had drifted farther and farther away from the liner, and then the liner had exploded.

"What are we going to do?" Billy asked again. Jimmy turned around and looked at his brother. Jimmy said nothing. Standing with his back to the control panel, Jimmy looked around the tiny room. On the gray metal walls were two portholes made of heavy plastic. Jimmy looked out through the one to his right. The stars looked cold.

There were eight children altogether. Besides Billy and himself, there were Tammy Wong and her brother, Jack; a little boy named Frankie; Patty and Sammy Gold; and the youngest, Albert Cohen.

"Sit still, all of you!" Jimmy said suddenly. "I'm going to check the controls now, so be quiet."

Jimmy turned and sat down in the control seat. All the lights on the panel were on—except one. The small sign under it read: *Emergency Sighting Light. When this light turns green, you are near a rescue ship. Push button to return signal.* This way Jimmy would know when help was near.

Then Jimmy saw a button with the word *Screen* under it. He pushed the button, and a screen lit up showing a picture of space. Jimmy couldn't understand the other buttons. "If only the ship's officer were here," Jimmy thought.

As Jimmy got up from the control seat, he thought of food. "How much is there?" he wondered. Slowly, he made his way back to the back of the control room. He opened the door to the ship's kitchen. He found dozens of cans of food, plus many large tanks of drinking water. Jimmy had no idea how long the food and water might last.

The tiny control room had four bunks that opened down from the wall. Jimmy's seven passengers climbed into the bunks to sleep. Jimmy watched them from the control seat, where he planned to sleep. "Soon," he thought, "their parents will be wondering what has happened to them. Well, I'm the oldest, and I'll take care of them."

The next day, Jimmy went into the kitchen to get some food. Billy followed him. "What's going to happen to us, Jimmy?" he asked.

"Wait, Billy. Don't ask me now."

By the sixth day after the wreck of the liner, Jimmy still tried not to show that he was scared. The food was going much faster than he had thought it would. There was still plenty of water, but in nine or ten days, all the food would be gone. "What will I do then?" Jimmy wondered. "What will I tell the others?"

Jimmy kept watching the emergency sighting light, hoping that it would come on. It never did. It was always dark. When he looked up at the screen, Jimmy saw that the stars had not changed.

On the thirteenth day, Jimmy woke up slowly. The others had been awake for some time, but they were still lying in their bunks. They had stopped playing a long time ago, it seemed. While some of them cried, others stayed quiet.

Jimmy got up and went to the kitchen for some food. When he saw that there was only enough left for three more days, he thought he would have to stop eating. He was bigger and stronger than the others. They needed the food more than he did.

Jimmy gave everyone some food. No one noticed that he took nothing.

When the lifeboat had been in space for seventeen days, the eight children inside were hungry and weak. There was no more food left from the dozens of cans that had been there. While the others cried, Jimmy thought about how happy he had been during the vacation on Lea. Everyone had laughed then. All that was gone now, as if it had never been.

With tears in his eyes, Jimmy looked up at the screen. Nothing had changed. "No one will come for us out of that darkness," Jimmy thought. "There are too many stars for us to get lost in."

Suddenly, Jimmy thought he saw the green light go on. "Do something, Jimmy!" shouted Billy. Jimmy leaned forward and pushed the button. As he watched the screen, waiting to see the rescue ship, he thought the stars looked almost friendly now. Jimmy looked at the screen. There was the rescue ship. Everything would soon be over.

1. What was Jimmy hoping to see when he looked at the screen?

2. What were some of the problems the children had on the lifeboat?

3. How did Jimmy know the rescue ship was coming?

4. Do you think Jimmy could have handled the situation differently? How?

5. When did you know the children were on their own in the lifeboat?

6. Jimmy was the oldest. How did he show that he felt responsible for the other children?

Think and Write

Prewrite

Jimmy was in a very difficult spot as the oldest on the spaceship's lifeboat. Imagine yourself in an emergency situation where you would have to lead a group of younger children out of trouble. What is the situation? How will you save the children? Write down a few ideas.

Draft

Now, use your ideas to write a good description of the emergency situation in which you have found yourself. Then, in another paragraph, explain how you will save the day! What will you do to get yourself and your friends out of trouble? Although your story is imaginary, try to make it seem real.

Revise

What you have written is fiction. Good fiction seems as if it could really happen. It is believable. Share your story with a classmate and check each other's stories to make sure there are details and information that make your stories seem real enough. Make necessary changes and work on your story to make sure it seems possible and real.

Context Clues

Astronauts have exciting jobs as space travelers.

What does the word *astronauts* mean? If you did not know the meaning of *astronauts,* what words in the sentence might help you? Notice the words *space travelers* in the sentence. These words help you know that astronauts are people who travel in space. The context, the other words in the sentence, gave you the clue to the meaning of *astronauts.*

Context clues may be in the same sentence as the word, or they may be in other sentences around the word. Read the sentences that follow.

Maria visited a space museum with her class and saw many kinds of spaceships. She liked the exhibit of rockets best.

If you did not know the meaning of *rockets,* other words around it would help you. The words *space museum* tell you that the rockets were in a museum for space objects. The words *many kinds of space-ships* tell you that rockets are a kind of spaceship.

Sometimes a definition may be given in the same sentence as the word. Words such as *is, means, meant, called,* and *or* often signal that a definition is going to be given. Read the following sentences. What does *astronomy* mean? How do you know?

- Astronomy is the study of the stars, planets, and other heavenly bodies.

- Astronomy means "the study of the stars, planets, and other heavenly bodies."

- The study of the stars, planets, and other heavenly bodies, called astronomy, is of great interest to him.

- The study of the stars, planets, and other heavenly bodies, or astronomy, is of great interest to her.

Each sentence gives the definition of *astronomy.* The words *is, means, called,* and *or* are clues that the sentence context contains the definition.

Textbook Application: Using Context Clues in Science

Many of the words in a science book are defined or explained in the context. Read the following article from a science book. Use the sidenotes to help you.

These two sentences help you know what planets are.

The context of this sentence defines *solar system.*

What is the meaning of the word *orbit*? What word signals that definition?

You are in a spaceship far out in space. In the distance, you can see the Sun. It glows with a bright yellow light. Near the Sun are nine other bodies in space. These bodies are called planets. The planets move around the Sun. They spin like tops, too. The Sun and the planets make up our solar system.

Each planet that you see is traveling around the Sun. Each travels in its own path, called an orbit. Some planets travel fast. Others travel slowly. They take a long, long time to complete one orbit around the Sun. Our journey starts now. Our ship will travel through the solar system.

—HBJ Science, Harcourt Brace Jovanovich

Read the paragraph that follows. Use context clues to find out the meaning of the words *astronomer, telescope, satellites,* and *comets.* Notice that signal words are given for some of the context clues.

A person who studies the objects in the night sky is an astronomer. An astronomer uses a telescope to see far into the distance. This instrument makes the stars and planets look bigger. Some of the planets have satellites, or moons, around them. Sometimes astronomers see frozen bodies of dust called comets.

Did you notice that signal words were given to help you know the meaning of *astronomer, satellites,* and *comets?* Did you also notice that no signal words were given for the meaning of *telescope?* The context of the second and third sentences helps you know the meaning of *telescope.* The clues in these sentences are *to see far into the distance* and *instrument makes the stars and planets look bigger.*

As you read and come to a word whose meaning you are not sure of, remember to look for context clues. Remember that context clues may be in the same sentence as the word, or they may be in other sentences around the word.

New York Times Best Illustrated
Children's Book

Who is Galileo Galilei?[1] Read to find out why he is still remembered today.

Galileo

by Arthur S. Gregor

From the time Galileo Galilei was a little boy, almost four hundred years ago, he thought about the stars and wondered about them. Even Galileo's father, who let him stay up late to look at the sky, filled with thousands of stars, couldn't answer all of his questions.

---

[1] Galileo Galilei [gal′ə•lē′ō gal′ə•lā′ē]

"There's the Milky Way," young Galileo cried, pointing to a great white cloud that stretched across the sky.

"What are the stars made of? Where did they come from? Will they go away?"

His father laughed. "Always asking questions, aren't you? When you are a student, you will read the books of those who are wise. There you will find some of the answers."

Galileo was a very good student. When he was seventeen years old, he went from Florence, Italy, to the city of Pisa[2] to study medicine. Galileo liked to ask questions about many things he saw around him. He soon realized that he did not want to be a doctor. He knew he wanted to be a scientist, but he would take no man's word without proof. Galileo became the first great scientist to rely chiefly on his own experiments.

In 1589, Galileo became a professor of mathematics at the University of Pisa, but he kept on with his experiments. For some time he had been thinking about what happens to objects as they fall. Do they fall at the same speed? Do they speed up? Can the speed be measured?

In order to be certain of his answers, Galileo thought he must slow down the fall. How?

---

[2] Pisa [pē′zə]

Then an idea came to him. Let a ball roll down a slope. If you could measure its speed, you could use the information for something that fell straight down.

After timing the speed of a rolling ball again and again, Galileo worked out two laws of motion. The first law he proved is that the longer something takes to fall, the faster it will go. The second law he proved is that the farther something has to drop, the faster it will fall. This is because its speed is always increasing.

In science, one discovery will often open the door to another. In the rolling-ball experiment, Galileo had noticed that when a ball reached the floor, it did not stop but kept on going for a while.

Galileo began to question himself. "What would happen if nothing got in the way of the ball?"

Galileo came to the idea that it would keep on going. He thought it would go out of the room, out of Pisa, out of Italy, and around the world forever.

Galileo's mind jumped from thinking about the earth to thinking about the moon, the sun, the stars, and the planets. Could it be possible that all of these were in motion because out in space there was nothing in the way? Galileo proved that things in space did move because there was nothing to get in their way.

When Galileo announced this idea to the world it created an uproar. Many professors at the University of Pisa did not believe Galileo. Galileo decided to leave

Pisa and go to Padua[3] to teach there.

In 1604, something happened that changed Galileo's life. A new star appeared in the sky. It glowed yellow, purple, red, and white. It was so bright it could be seen during the day. The star shone for one-and-one-half years. Then it faded and disappeared. People who lived at that time did not think the universe could change. They thought that new stars could not appear. Galileo did not agree with the people who thought that the universe did not change. Everyone wondered how he could be certain when everything was so far away.

Today we know that the new star was a supernova. A supernova is a star that explodes like a giant firework and scatters its pieces over the sky. There have been only four supernovas in the last thousand years. Galileo lived to see two of them.

---

[3] Padua [paj′o͞o•ə]

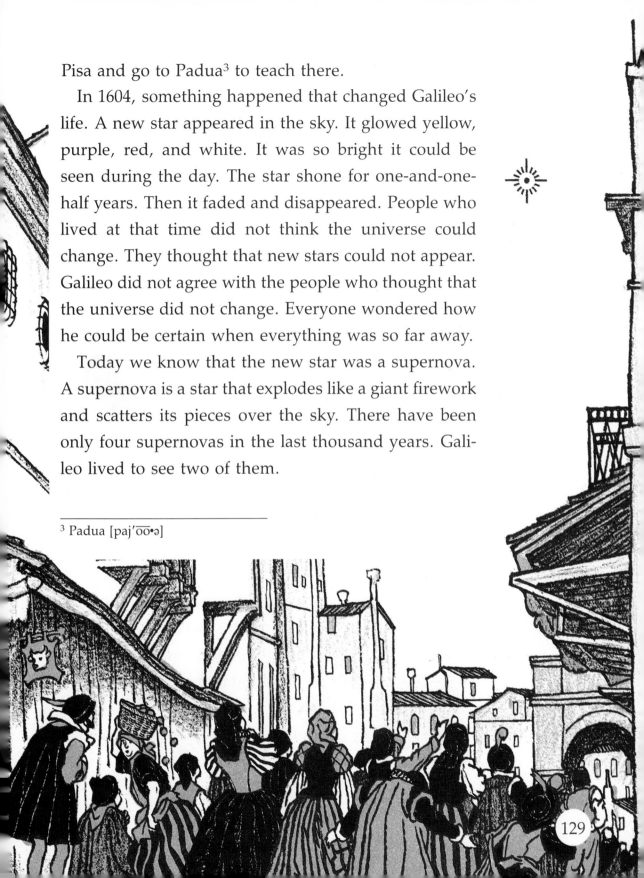

In 1609, Galileo built his own telescope. It brought things three times closer to the earth. This made it easier for Galileo to see things in the universe. Later he built another telescope that brought things in the universe thirty times closer to the earth. Then people saw parts of the sky that had never been seen before.

With the new telescope, Galileo made many discoveries. He found that the Milky Way was not a cloud, but a great cluster of stars. Each star was too small to be seen with the eye alone.

Galileo discovered that the moon was not perfectly smooth and it was not perfectly round. It was creased and had deep craters.

One night while looking through his telescope Galileo picked out what seemed to be three small stars very close to the planet Jupiter. Unlike stars, these kept moving from one side of the planet to the other. A few weeks later Galileo found a fourth jumpy little body near the others. He had never seen a star that acted that way before. Galileo discovered that these were not stars at all. They were moons traveling around Jupiter just as our moon goes around the earth.

Galileo returned to Florence. He began talking about another discovery. Galileo found that the planet Venus seems to change its shape.

There could be only one explanation. Venus was not going around the earth. It circled the sun! This was

proof that Copernicus[4] was right. Copernicus was the first man in modern times to state that the earth went around the sun. Galileo was one of the few people who believed Copernicus.

To tell the world about his new discoveries Galileo wrote a book called *The Two Chief Systems.* He wrote in Italian, the language of the people, so that every man and woman would understand.

Galileo knew his work was just a beginning. He knew that some day others would explore the rest of the universe. Galileo was right. Today there are astronomers who are studying outer space and are using Galileo's discoveries. The astronauts, too, depend on the first great scientist of modern times—Galileo Galilei.

---

[4] Copernicus [kə•pûr′nə•kəs]

1. Why is Galileo's work still important today?

2. What did Galileo do that made him famous?

3. How does Galileo's discovery that things move in space help us today?

4. What do you think about Galileo's discoveries?

5. What told you that Galileo was able to prove that the universe changes?

6. What questions did Galileo have about the universe, and how did he find the answers?

Prewrite

With a classmate, look back over the story to find several different words that were defined by *context clues.* Together, make a list of these words. Look at exactly how the author does this. For example, look for the word *astronomer* and see how the author has told the reader something about astronomers. Complete the following chart with the information you find.

Words	Context Clues
astronomers	study outer space

Draft

Select a word from your chart and write a paragraph that will help the reader to know more about the word. Like the author, try to write and use *context clues* in interesting ways.

Revise

Exchange paragraphs with a classmate. Write two questions about each other's topic. Then use the two questions that your partner wrote to revise your paragraph. Make sure that the new information works well in your paragraph.

My Star

by Marion Kennedy

In a sky of black velvet
The silver stars shine.
I think I'll choose one
And pretend it is mine.
I'll choose one that twinkles
And winks down at me;
Then snug in my bed every
Night I shall see
My very own star shining
Far overhead,
And winking good night to me,
Curled up in bed.

135

How does the boy in this story learn that his dad "really is something"?

My Dad Is Really Something

by Lois Osborn

Ron is a new boy in my class. I like him a lot, but sometimes he makes me mad.

One day I showed the kids at school a book my dad had written. Then Ron had to speak up.

"Aw, that's nothing, Harry George," he said. "You should see what my father can do. He can tear a phone book in half with his bare hands. I bet your father can't do that."

When I got home, I gave the phone book to my dad. I told him what Ron's father could do.

"How about you?" I asked.

He shook his head. "I'm no strong man, Harry George," he said. I put the phone book away. He could at least have tried.

Then I remembered how once my mom and I had watched my dad climb a tall ladder, crawl up the roof, hang onto a chimney, and reach way out to rescue my kitten. We were scared my dad would fall. Maybe my dad isn't real strong, but he sure is brave. So I told Ron all about what my dad had done.

"Aw, that's nothing, Harry George," Ron said. He was not impressed. "My father fought in the war. He has a whole box full of medals he won for bravery."

After school, I watched my dad fix my bike. I looked at all the tools in his box. I wished they were medals.

"How come you never fought in the war?" I casually asked my dad.

"Flat feet and poor eyesight," my dad said. "They couldn't use me. I was lucky."

"Lucky?" I exclaimed. "You could've won a lot of medals, like Ron's father."

"Ron's father?" my dad said. "Oh, I remember him. The fellow who tears up telephone books. So he won medals, did he?"

"For bravery," I explained.

"Well, good for him," said my dad, and he shut his tool box with a bang.

Later, my dad and I finished the model plane we had been working on. I could hardly wait to show it to Ron.

"See what my dad and I made?" I said to him. "I bet you and your father never made anything like this."

"Aw, that's nothing, Harry George," Ron answered. "My father doesn't fool around with model planes. He flies real ones instead. The kind that take off and land on a carrier. That's dangerous stuff!"

As soon as I got home, I asked my dad if he would like to be a pilot.

"I don't care that much about flying," he told me.

"Why not?" I asked.

"Well, let's just say I feel better getting off a plane than I do getting on."

I wished he hadn't said that. I started to walk away.

"Wait a minute," said my dad. "Does Ron's father happen to be an airline pilot?"

"Oh no," I replied. "He flies fighter jets on carriers for the Navy."

"That figures," I heard my dad mutter.

139

The next evening, there was an open house at school. I went with my mom and dad. They looked at my work and talked to my teacher.

"Is Ron's father here?" my dad casually asked her. "Harry George is really impressed with him. I'd like to meet him."

My teacher looked at me in surprise.

"You must be thinking of someone else," she said. "Ron's father died years ago."

I walked home like a robot. I couldn't talk or think. "How could Ron do that to me?" I asked. "We were friends. Why did he have to lie to me?"

"Maybe it didn't seem like lying to Ron," my dad said.

"All that junk about tearing the telephone book," I said, "and the medals, and flying a plane. All lies! I believed him. I can never be friends with him again. Never!"

I turned my back and walked out of the kitchen. I wondered what it would be like to have a make-believe father instead of a real dad like mine. I'm glad my dad is real.

The next morning I told my dad that maybe I'd be friends with Ron after all. That's how the three of us began doing things together.

At recess today, I heard Ron say to some kids, "Harry George's father takes us fishing. He knows ten different ways to make paper airplanes. Harry George's father is really something."

Yes, that's my dad, all right. He is really something!

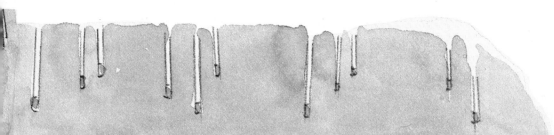

1. What did Harry George learn about his dad?

2. Why did Ron brag about his father?

3. Whom did Ron brag about at the end of the story?

4. Did your feelings about Ron change as you read the story? Why?

5. When did you know that Harry George thought his dad was "really something"?

6. How does Harry George's opinion of his father change from the beginning to the end of the story?

Prewrite

In stories, you can learn about the characters by what they say and do. In this story you learned a lot about Ron, Harry George, and Harry George's father. Choose one of these characters and look back over the story at things the character did that let you know more about him.

Then complete the following web with information about the character. Write words that describe the character in the small circles.

Draft

Write a character sketch about the character you have selected. Tell about the person and use things that the person did in the story to back up your description. Try to give a good, solid description that shows the kind of person the character is.

Revise

Look over the story for more information that you might want to give about the character you chose. Is there more you could add to make it a better character sketch? Have you used things that the characters actually did in the story to back up your description? Improve your story if you can.

Thinking About "Portholes"

People's views can change, and some of the characters in "Portholes" are proof of that. Remember that Elisabeth followed clues and discovered that the beach holds many different kinds of treasures.

Jimmy Wilson didn't let the other children know that he was scared. What caused him to have a different view of the situation?

What Galileo saw through his telescope changed the way everyone sees the Earth, the moon, the sun, the stars, and the planets. His discoveries have changed the way scientists view the universe.

You read how Harry George's idea of his father changed. At first he felt bad when he compared his dad to another boy's father, but then he learned that his father was "really something."

As you read other stories, watch the characters closely. Notice what happens and see if the characters are the same at the end of the story as they seemed to be in the beginning. Ask yourself why the characters change.

1. Both Miss Moody and Jimmy faced dangerous situations. Explain each situation and tell how each character changed his or her viewpoint as a result.

2. How are Miss Moody, Jimmy, and Galileo alike? How are they different?

3. Which character, Miss Moody or Elisabeth, did not change the way she viewed the beach? Explain your answer.

4. How are Harry George's idea of his father and Elisabeth's idea of her father different?

5. Which character seemed to you to change the most? Why do you think so?

Unit 3
Beauty

Have you ever thought about the kinds of beauty that surround you? There is beauty found in nature. Think about the flowers that grow wild on hillsides or those that are planted in neat rows in a park.

An artist creates another kind of beauty by adding color with brushes and paint. Think about how musicians and writers create beautiful sounds and stories. They express what they think and feel through notes and words. Everyone can make the world a more beautiful place to live.

The characters in this unit invite you to join them as they add beauty to their worlds. As you read, think about how each of the characters tries to make the world a better place.

Read on Your Own

Dancing Is *by George Ancona. Dutton.* Photographs of all kinds of dancers from all over the world show us how people enjoy dancing.

My Friend the Monster *by Clyde Robert Bulla. Crowell.* A plain-looking prince is hidden away by his parents and finds a secret friend in an ugly monster.

Seeds by Wind and Water *by Helene Jordan. Harper.* Seeds travel in many ways. Wind and water, dogs and cats, and even the tires of cars and planes carry seeds from place to place.

Happy Birthday, Grampie *by Susan Pearson. Dial.* Martha makes Grampie a beautiful birthday card with raised felt letters so that he can "see" it even though he is blind.

Abiyoyo: Based on a South African Lullaby *by Pete Seeger. Macmillan.* A fearsome giant is destroyed by a beautiful song about himself.

How the First Rainbow Was Made *by Ruth Robbins. Houghton.* The rain must be stopped, so coyote gathers the others and they visit Old-Man-Above. He rewards them by creating a rainbow.

The Happy Funeral *by Eve Bunting. Harper.* Laura is sad over the death of her grandfather. The beautiful customs of her Chinese-American family help her overcome her grief.

The Gift *by Helen Coutant. Knopf.* A young Vietnamese-American girl cannot decide on a gift for a blind elderly friend and finally brings the joy of the beauty she has seen that day.

The Reward Worth Having *by Jay Williams. Four Winds.* Three soldiers are rewarded for their helpfulness and can choose the thing each wants most.

Evan's Corner *by Elizabeth Starr Hill. Holt.* Evan wants his own space and fixes up a corner to his liking. Later he finds that he is happier when he helps his younger brother fix a space for himself.

A Wizard tries to make the world more beautiful. How does he do this?

The Great Blueness

story and pictures by Arnold Lobel

Long ago there were no colors in the world at all. Almost everything was gray, and what was not gray was black or white. It was a time that was called The Great Grayness.

Every morning a Wizard who lived during the time of The Great Grayness would open his window to look out at the wide land.

"Something is very wrong with the world," he would say. "It is hard to tell when the rainy days stop and the sunny days begin."

150

The Wizard would often go down the stairs to his dark, gray cellar. There, just to amuse himself and to forget about the drab world outside, he would make wonderful magic potions and spells.

One day while the Wizard was mixing and stirring a little of this and a bit of that, he saw something strange in the bottom of his pot.

"What good-looking stuff I have made!" he exclaimed. "I will make some more right away."

"What is it?" asked the neighbors when they saw the Wizard painting his house.

"A color," said the Wizard. "I call it *blue*."

"Please," cried the neighbors, "please give us some!"

"Of course," said the Wizard.

And that was how The Great Blueness came to be. After a short time everything in the world was blue. Trees were blue. Bees were blue. Wheels and evening meals were blue. The Wizard would pedal out on his blue bicycle to look around at the wide, blue world. He would say, "What a perfect day we are having."

But The Blueness was not so perfect. After a long time all that blue made everyone sad. Children played no games. They sulked in their blue backyards. Mothers and fathers sat at home and stared gloomily at the blue pictures on the walls of their blue living rooms.

"This Blueness is too depressing," said the neighbors to the Wizard, who was unhappier than anyone.

"Nobody laughs anymore," he said. "Even I myself have not smiled for days. I must do something," said the Wizard as he slouched down the stairs to his dark, blue cellar. There he began to mix and stir a little of this and a bit of that. Soon he saw something new in the bottom of his pot.

"Now here is happier stuff," said the Wizard. "I will make some more right away."

"What is that?" asked the neighbors when they saw the Wizard painting his fence.

"I am calling it *yellow*," said the Wizard.

"May we have some?" begged the neighbors.

"You may," replied the Wizard.

And that was how The Great Yellowness came to be.
After a short time everything in the world was yellow.
There was not a flyspeck of blue anywhere to be seen.
Pigs were yellow. Wigs were yellow. Stairs and dentist
chairs were yellow. The Wizard would gallop out on his
yellow horse to explore the wide, yellow world. He
would say, "What a fine day we are having."

But The Yellowness was not so fine. After a long time all that yellow began to hurt everyone's eyes. People walked about bumping and thumping into each other. They were squinting and could not see where they were going.

"This Yellowness is too bright and blinding," said the neighbors to the Wizard.

"You don't have to tell me," moaned the Wizard, who had a cold towel on his head. "Everyone has a headache, and so do I."

So the Wizard stumbled down the stairs to his dark, yellow cellar. There he mixed and stirred a little of this and a bit of that. Soon he saw something different in the bottom of his pot.

"This is handsome stuff," declared the Wizard. "I will make some more right away."

"What do you call that?" asked the neighbors when they saw the Wizard painting his flowers.

"*Red*," answered the Wizard.

"We would like some too," pleaded the neighbors.

"Right away," said the Wizard.

That was how The Great Redness came to be. After a short time everything in the world was red. Mountains were red. Fountains were red. Cheese and afternoon teas were red. The Wizard would sail out in his red boat

to see what he could see of the wide, red world. He
would say, "What a glorious day we are having."

But The Redness was not so glorious. After a long
time all that red put everyone into a very bad temper.
Children spent their days fighting and punching each
other while mothers and fathers argued loudly. A furious
crowd of neighbors marched to the Wizard's house.

"This awful Redness is all your fault," they shouted.

The Wizard stormed down the stairs to his dark, red
cellar. He mixed and stirred for many days. He used all
the magic that he could think of to find a new color, but
all that he made was more blue, more yellow, and more
red. The Wizard worked until all of his pots were filled
to the top.

155

The pots were so full that they soon overflowed. The blue and the yellow and the red all began to mix together. It was a terrible mess. But when the Wizard saw what was happening, he exclaimed, "That is the answer!" And he danced joyfully around the cellar.

The Wizard mixed the red with the blue and made a new color. Then he mixed the yellow with the blue and made a new color. The Wizard mixed the yellow with the red and made a new color.

"Hurrah!" he shouted, and he mixed the red and the blue and the yellow in all kinds of different ways.

"Look at these beautiful things I have made!" said the Wizard when he was finished.

"What are they?" asked the neighbors.

"I call them purple and green and orange and brown," said the Wizard.

"They are a sight for sore eyes," cried the neighbors, "but which one shall we choose this time?"

"You must take them all," said the Wizard.

The people did take all the colors the Wizard had made. After a short time they found good places for each one. And after a long time when the Wizard opened his window, he would look out and say, "What a perfectly fine and glorious day we are having!"

The neighbors brought the Wizard gifts of red apples and green leaves and yellow bananas and purple grapes and blue flowers. At last the world was too beautiful ever to be changed again.

1. How did the Wizard make the world more beautiful?

2. What happened when everything in the world was painted blue? Yellow? Red?

3. How did the Wizard solve these problems about color?

4. Would you choose a blue, yellow, or red world to live in? Why?

5. When did you know the world would soon be colorful?

6. How would your world be different if there were no colors?

Think and Write

Prewrite

Look at the colors around you right now. Think about how different colors make you feel. Think about how color adds to the beauty of the world around us. Copy and complete the following chart as you think about each color.

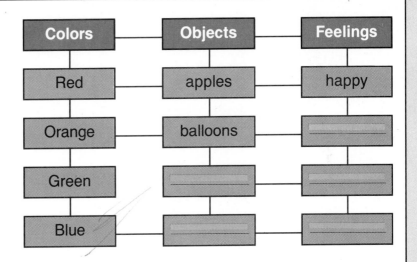

Colors	Objects	Feelings
Red	apples	happy
Orange	balloons	___
Green	___	___
Blue	___	___

Draft

Write about your favorite color. Start your story by explaining how your favorite color makes you feel. For example, "I feel calm when I am wearing blue." Describe at least three things that are this color. End your story by telling why you like that color. Don't forget to use the information on your chart.

Revise

Does your first sentence tell the reader a feeling? Does your story give the reader a strong sense of why you like the color? If the answer to either of these questions is no, change your story.

The Colors Live
by Mary O'Neill

The Colors live
Between black and white
In a land that we
Know best by sight.
But knowing best
Isn't everything,
For colors dance
And colors sing,
And colors laugh
And colors cry—
Turn off the light
And colors die,
And they make you feel
Every feeling there is
From the grumpiest grump
To the fizziest fizz.
And you and you and I
Know well
Each has a taste
And each has a smell
And each has a wonderful
Story to tell. . . .

Draw Conclusions

Sometimes an author leaves out important information from a story. In order to decide what has happened, you have to think about what you already know about the topic. You also need to think about the information the author has given.

Read the following paragraph taken from "The Great Blueness."

The pots were so full that they soon overflowed. The blue and the yellow and the red all began to mix together. It was a terrible mess. But when the Wizard saw what was happening, he exclaimed, "That is the answer!" And he danced joyfully around the cellar.

What do you think happened in the paragraph? You may have used the information in the paragraph to decide that the blue, yellow, and red colors mixed together. You also may have used information you already knew about colors to decide that when the three primary colors mixed together, they formed all the other colors. When you do this, you are **drawing conclusions** from the information given in the story and from what you already know about colors.

Now read the paragraph below and decide what has happened.

Harry George and Ron were doing their homework together one night. They heard thunder nearby and saw a streak of lightning in the sky. Suddenly the lights went out in the house. The boys ran to the window and noticed that there were no street lights shining. They could not see any lights burning in the windows of the houses in the neighborhood.

What conclusion could you draw about what has happened in the paragraph? If you decide that the electricity went out in the area because of the storm, you are drawing conclusions from what you read and from what you already know about storms.

As you read, remember to use the information that is given and what you already know about the topic to draw conclusions and discover what has happened.

Beauty can be heard as well as seen. How does a one-man band bring beauty to a town?

Ty's One-man Band

by Mildred Pitts Walter

The sun rose aflame. It quickly dried the dew and baked the town. Another hot, humdrum day. Ty's mother was washing clothes, and his father was busy unloading feed for the chickens. His sister was in the kitchen. Ty had nothing fun to do.

Ty thought of the tall cool grass at the pond and decided to go there.

At the pond, big trees sank their roots down deep and lifted their branches up, up, toward the sky. The grass grew tall enough to hide a boy as big as Ty. He lay quiet, listening. Step-th-hump . . . Ty pressed his ear to the ground. He heard it again: step-th-hump, step-th-hump, step-th-hump. What could it be? Step-th-hump, step-th-hump, closer it came. Then Ty saw a man with only one leg. The other leg was a wooden peg.

The man walked to the water's edge and set a bundle down. He took out a tin cup, a tin plate, a

spoon, and some food. After he ate, he washed his dishes in the pond. Then the man tossed the cup, plate, and spoon in the air one after the other, over and over and over and caught them all. "He's a juggler!" Ty thought. Then the man beat a rhythm with the spoon on the cup: tink-ki-tink-ki-ki-tink-ki-tink; and on the plate: tank-ka-tank-ka-ka-tank-ka-tank; and then on the cup and plate: tink-ki-tink-ki-tank.

"He's a drummer, too," Ty said to himself. Ty walked closer to the man. Ty felt his heart beat: thump, thump.

The sun turned into a glowing red ball. It sank lower and lower, but the town didn't cool. People fanned themselves on their porches. It was so hot they didn't even talk.

Ty sat under a street lamp in the town square. He waited. Would Andro come? And if he came, what kind of music would he make with Jason's comb, the old washboard, two wooden spoons, and a pail?

Then in the darkness he heard a step-th-hump, step-th-hump, step-th-hump. Andro was coming!

"I'm here at your service," said Andro. Andro looked at all the things. He turned them about one by one. "These will make fine music," he said as he sat with his good leg folded under him. He placed the spoons between his fingers, and he moved them very fast. Quack-quack-quacket-t-quack. The empty square filled with the sound of ducks.

Then Andro made the sound of horses dancing slowly, Clip-clop-clip-clop-clop. They danced faster, clipty-clop, clipty-clop, clipty-clop-clop. Faster still, cl-oo-py, cl-oo-pop, cl-oo-pop-pop-pop-pop-pop. "Hi ho, Silver!" Andro shouted.

Ty clapped and clapped. Andro took a thin piece of tissue paper from his pocket. Carefully he folded the tissue paper over the comb. Before Ty could ask what that was all about, Andro was making music.

One by one people began to leave their porches. They pressed in closer and clapped their hands and tapped their feet in rhythm as Andro played and danced to his own music. His peg leg went tap-tap-ti-ti-tappity-tap, tappity-tap-tap-ti-ti-tap. He twirled, skipped, and danced 'round and 'round in the spotlight of the street lamp.

Andro stopped dancing and began to make sounds on the washboard. As he passed his fingers over the board, Andro made many sounds that Ty thought sounded very real. Ty could hear water falling, rushing down a hill over rocks, then gurgling in a stream, and then trickling to a drip, like from a faucet. Best of all were sounds of a big freight train puffing slowly, then faster, faster, faster still, then passing by with the whistle far away.

"More! More! More!" the people shouted.

Andro set the pail down. With a spoon in his hand, he hit the pail, his wooden leg, and the other spoon. Di-de-le-dum, di-de-le-dum, de-di-la-di-ti-do, de-di-la-de-ti-do, chuck-chick-chu-dum, chuck-chick-chu-dum.

Boys and girls, mothers and fathers, even the babies clapped their hands. Some danced and twirled in the street. Whenever the music stopped, everybody shouted, "More!"

Andro let Ty take turns using the instruments. Ty's friends wanted turns, too. Soon they played together like a one-man band. Everybody danced. Only Ty saw Andro slip away back into the night.

171

1. How does a one-man band bring beauty to a town?

2. Why did Ty gather all the things that Andro asked him to get?

3. Why was it good for the town when Andro came?

4. What did you think when Andro slipped away unseen into the night?

5. When did you know that Andro had changed the town?

6. Name the ways Andro created music.

Prewrite

Listen to the sounds around you right now. Listen to the sounds in the hall or the sounds outside the building. Like color, sound is an important part of our world. Good writers help you to see stories and to hear the sounds of their stories. Think about some enjoyable and exciting sounds you have heard in your life.

Where did you hear them? What did they sound like?

Draft

Write a story about something that you have done, something that has happened to you, or somewhere you have been. Use sound words to help the reader get more feeling from your story. Include in your story sounds you have heard or might hear.

Revise

Check over your story for sound words. Will the reader have a good sense of what you heard when the story happened? Be careful not to overdo the sounds. Read your story aloud to a classmate and ask him or her to repeat or tell you the sounds he or she heard in your story. Add more appropriate sounds if you need to improve your story.

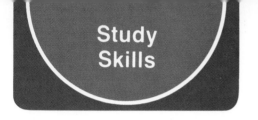

Follow Directions
Make Musical Instruments

Ty and his friends made simple musical instruments from pots, pails, a washboard, a comb, and other household items. By following directions, you can learn how to make some simple musical instruments. Then you can have your own class band.

Here are some important things to keep in mind when following written directions:

- Be sure to read all the steps very carefully. Then read them again. Make sure you understand what you are to do.
- Gather together the things you will need.
- Begin with step 1 of the directions and follow all the steps in order. Be sure not to leave out any of the steps.

A kazoo is one simple instrument that you can make.

Things you will need:
    wax paper
    scissors
    a 5-inch, or 12-cm, cardboard tube
    a rubber band

1. Cut out about a 6-inch, or 15-cm, circle of wax paper.

2. Put the wax paper over one end of the tube.

3. Wrap the rubber band tightly around the wax paper to hold it in place on the tube.

4. Hum a tune into the open end of the tube. The kazoo will change your voice to make a buzzing sound.

Now follow these directions to make a comb harmonica.

Things you will need:
scissors
a small, clean comb
a piece of wax paper or tissue paper

1. Cut the wax paper or tissue paper so that it is the same length as the comb. Make sure the paper is wide enough to cover both sides of the teeth of the comb.

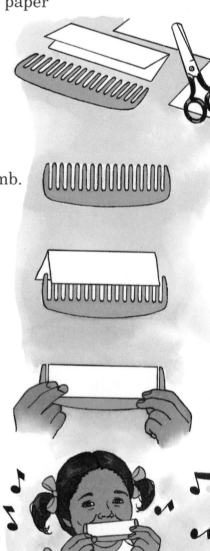

2. Hold the comb so the teeth are pointing up.

3. Fold the wax paper or tissue paper over the top of the teeth.

4. Hold the wax paper or tissue paper on the comb at both ends.

5. Put your mouth against one side of the paper-covered comb and hum into the comb.

Here are directions for making a rubber-band guitar.

Things you will need:
empty tissue box
four or five rubber bands
two 6-inch, or 15-cm, wooden dowels or
two unsharpened pencils

1. Put the rubber bands around the tissue box and across the opening.

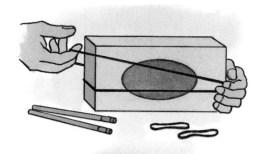

2. Put the pencils under the rubber bands on either side of the opening in the tissue box.

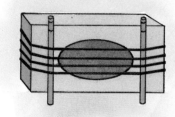

3. Now try playing your guitar by plucking the rubber band strings.

Now you have made three simple instruments. Try playing them with other members of your class.

Beauty means different things to different people. What does beauty mean to the Queen? What does the Mirror have to say about beauty?

Snow White and Friends

by Val R. Cheatham

CHARACTERS:

Narrator	Woodsman
Queen	Doc
Snow White	Dopey
Mirror	

SCENE 1

Setting: The Queen's throne room. Mirror is placed near throne. The Narrator enters and speaks.

Narrator: This play is about a little girl who grew up and became beautiful. Her name is Snow White. As the scene opens, we see the wicked Queen. (*Queen enters.*)

Adapted from *Skits and Spoofs for Young Actors* by Val R. Cheatham. Copyright © 1977 by Val R. Cheatham. Published by Plays, Inc., Boston, MA. This play is for reading purposes only. For permission to perform, write to Plays, Inc., 120 Boylston Street, Boston, MA 02116. Reprinted by permission of Plays, Inc.

Queen: Tell me, Mirror, am I still the most lovely creature that ever lived?

Mirror: To hear the things I have to say, you must ask the proper way.

Queen: Oh, you and your rhymes!

Mirror: A looking glass is all I can be, when you forget to question me.

Queen: Oh, all right! All right! Who's the fairest of them all?

Mirror: There are some things, O my Queen, of which I joke a lot, but where your beauty is concerned, you know I kid you not! A lovely sight—young Snow White.

Queen: Snow White? I can't have this. For someone to be lovelier than I is out of the question. She must be done away with. I'll call the Woodsman!

Woodsman: *(entering)* You called?

Queen: Yes. I have a little job for you.

Woodsman: Chopping down trees?

Queen: Well, it's a kind of chopping.

Woodsman: Name it, my Queen. It shall be done.

Queen: You see, there's this girl, Snow White. She's more beautiful than I. Snow White must die because there can never be anyone else alive to equal my beauty.

Woodsman: You know getting rid of the girl is not my line of work.

Queen: You have a choice between two heads.

Woodsman: Two? One is enough!

Queen: A choice between two, Woodsman. Yours or the girl's. . . . Well?

Woodsman: Very well, my Queen. When you put it that way . . .

Queen: *(to Mirror)* Heh, heh, heh. How about that, Mirror-Mirror-on-the-wall?

SCENE 2

Setting: The forest.

Narrator: What will happen to young Snow White? In this scene, the Woodsman and Snow White are in the forest. *(Woodsman and Snow White enter; Narrator exits.)*

Woodsman: This, Snow White, is a pine tree.

Snow White: Oh! How very interesting.

Woodsman: Now, can you see what's over there?

Snow White: *(bending over and looking off)* Where?

Woodsman: *(prepares ax, then drops it on the ground)* I can't do it!

Snow White: Can't do what, Mr. Woodsman?

Woodsman: I can't obey the Queen. She sent me out here to get rid of you because of your beauty.

Snow White: Me? Why, only yesterday they were calling me the Ugly Duckling.

Woodsman: That was yesterday. You stay here, and I'll go tell the Queen you're dead.

Snow White: I'm concerned. Will that be safe for you, Mr. Woodsman?

Woodsman: I'll be all right. The Queen's getting old. Many girls are more beautiful than she is. Soon you will be able to go back. I must leave; be careful. *(Woodsman exits.)*

Snow White: Thank you and good-bye. Now, which way shall I go? *(looking off to the right)*

Doc and Dopey: *(enter)* Hi-ho, hi-ho . . .

Snow White: Oh, who are you?

Dopey: We're The Dwarfs.

Snow White: I'm supposed to meet The Seven Dwarfs, and they will take me home and help me.

Doc: That's our name: "The Seven Dwarfs—Littlest Band with the Biggest Beat." He's Dopey, and I'm Doc. Who are you?

Snow White: I'm Snow White. The wicked Queen wants me done away with because of my beauty.

Doc: Can you play drums?

Snow White: No. *(crying)* Oh, why does the Queen hate me so?

Dopey: The Queen doesn't like us either.

Doc: The Dwarfs had three hits on the top ten. We were getting to be more popular than the Queen, but she fixed that. She sent us to the woods. Now we only play for the sparrows and the blue jays.

Dopey: She said our music was for the birds.

Doc: Are you sure you're not a drummer?

Snow White: I'm really sure. But I can sing.

Doc: That's it! A singer! That could give our sound some real class. *(They exit.)*

SCENE 3

Setting: The Queen's throne room.

Narrator: For the next scene we go back to visit the Queen and her magic mirror. Will Snow White stay in the forest and sing with The Dwarfs? Will the Woodsman escape to the woods and become the new drummer for The Dwarfs? *(Mirror is on stage; Queen enters; Narrator exits.)*

Queen: *(looking into the mirror)* There can never be anyone with beauty equal to mine. Isn't that right, Mirror?

Mirror: To hear the things I have to say, you must ask the proper way.

Queen: All right, all right. I'll ask in rhyme. Mirror-Mirror-on-the-wall-who's-the-fairest-of-them-all? Now, hurry up and tell me.

Mirror: Raven hair as soft as silk, eyes so bright and blue, blushing sunshine in her cheeks, a heart so kind and true—

Queen: Wait a minute! Raven hair? You're not going to give me that Snow White speech again, are you? Remember? The Woodsman?

Mirror: Very much alive is Snow White, our lovely heroine. The tenderhearted Woodsman was too kind to do her in. She's taken cover with some dwarfs, who helped her in her flight. Now she's singing happy tunes with the little band each night.

Queen: Snow White is still alive! What's a queen to do when no one will obey her?

Mirror: Beauty is not meant to be one's only goal in life. It's courage, faith, and goodness that can help one get through life. These things will stay right with you; they can't be bought or sold. Beauty changes with the years, and, face it, Queen—you're old.

Queen: I must do something. I'll get rid of Snow White myself. I'll poison her. I'll take this nice, red, juicy *(pulls banana from pocket)* banana? Well, one thing will work as well as another. How about that, Mirror-Mirror-on-the-wall?

185

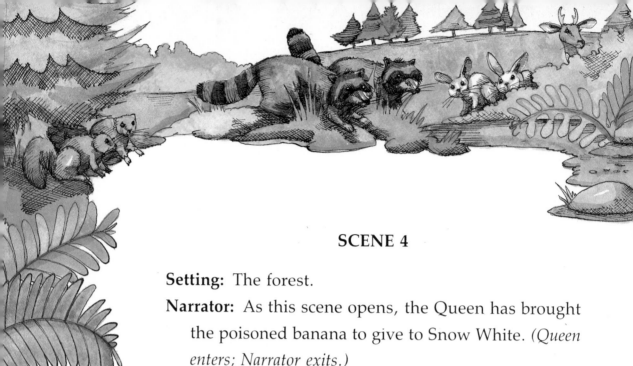

SCENE 4

Setting: The forest.

Narrator: As this scene opens, the Queen has brought the poisoned banana to give to Snow White. (*Queen enters; Narrator exits.*)

Queen: Oh, Snow White—where are you? Yoo-hoo! (*Snow White enters.*)

Snow White: Were you calling me?

Queen: Yes. You're such a cute little thing and do such a good job singing with the band, I want you to have this banana.

Snow White: You've heard my singing?

Queen: Yes, I've heard you. I used to do some singing myself. Here, have a banana.

Snow White: I really don't care for this banana.

Queen: But it's such a beauty, and I do want you to have it.

Snow White: All right, but I don't like bananas.

Queen: This one is . . . different. (*Snow White peels it and takes a bite; then she drops to floor.*) Let's hear you sing now! (*moves away from Snow White*)

Queen: *(Doc and Dopey enter.)* Hello, who are you?

Doc: Doc Dwarf, leader of The Seven Dwarfs. Would you like to come hear us play? *(takes apple from pocket)* Have an apple.

Queen: Thank you. *(Queen eats apple as she and Doc exit.)*

Dopey: *(turns and sees Snow White on the floor)* What's wrong with Snow White?

Woodsman: *(enters)* She is waiting for me! The Queen just gave her a poisoned banana, and I'm the Prince with the cure that will get our heroine back on her feet. Let's see—*(searches pockets, finds bottle)* Banana-cure! *(passes bottle under Snow White's nose)*

Snow White: *(sitting up and rubbing eyes)* You're the Woodsman.

Woodsman: Wrong! I am the Prince dressed as a tenderhearted Woodsman to escape from the Queen. But that's all ended now. Doc just gave her a Boy Scout Apple. One bite and she will act like a true Boy Scout. She will also feel like doing a good deed every day!

1. Why was the Queen such a mean person? What does beauty mean to the Queen?

2. What good things happened to Snow White because the Queen was jealous of her?

3. What happened to the Queen after Doc Dwarf gave her an apple?

4. Whose definition of beauty do you like better, the Queen's or the Mirror's? Why?

5. When did you know that Snow White's problems would be solved?

6. The Queen's idea of beauty is different from the Mirror's idea of beauty. What does beauty mean to you?

Prewrite

The author has written a funny play based on the fairy tale "Snow White and the Seven Dwarfs." She has used the basic story, but has changed what the characters say and some of the details to make the play funny. With a partner, think about

188

another fairy tale. What changes would you need to make if you wanted to rewrite that fairy tale as a funny play? Who would the characters be? What would the setting be?

Draft

With your partner, rewrite a fairy tale as a play. Use your own words and feel free to change the story to make your play funny and to make it fit into the present time. Look at how the author of "Snow White and Friends" has written what the characters say. Use this same form.

Revise

Read your play to two other classmates. Listen to their suggestions about what you might add or how you might change your play. Make the necessary changes.

Beauty

by E-Yeh-Shure'

Beauty is seen
In the sunlight,
The trees, the birds,
Corn growing and people working
Or dancing for their harvest.

Beauty is heard
In the night,
Wind sighing, rain falling,
Or a singer chanting
Anything in earnest.

Beauty is in yourself.
Good deeds, happy thoughts
That repeat themselves
In your dreams,
In your work,
And even in your rest.

Topic, Main Idea, and Details

Look at the picture. It shows something happening. What does the picture show? The picture is about gardening. "Gardening" is the **topic** of the picture. What is the most important thing the picture shows? *The children are planting a garden.* The **main idea** is that the children are planting a garden. Look to see what each child is doing. One is raking. Another is planting seeds. The last child is watering the garden. These are the details in the picture. All these details together are the **supporting details** for the main idea: *the children are planting a garden.*

Just as a picture can have a main idea, most of the paragraphs you read have main ideas, too. Read the paragraph below and find the main idea.

Seed plants grow in many different places. Some plants grow better in places that are hot while others grow better in cool places. Some need a great deal of sunlight; some grow best in shade. While some plants grow in very dry places, others can be found in very wet places. Some plants may even grow in water. Look in open fields, in gardens, in the cracks of sidewalks, and in flowerpots. You may find seed plants growing there.

What is the main idea? In this paragraph, the first sentence, *Seed plants grow in many different places,* states the main idea.

The main idea, however, will not always be the first sentence of the paragraph. Sometimes the main idea will not be in a sentence. You will have to summarize the information to understand what the main idea is. To find the main idea, first look for the topic of the paragraph. The topic is what the paragraph is about. The topic of the paragraph you just read is "seed plants." The main idea is the most important thing the paragraph says about the topic.

Now read the paragraph about seed plants once more. Look for the details that support the main idea.

Did you notice that every sentence tells you something about the different places that seed plants grow? Read the following list. It shows the details from the paragraph that support the main idea.

Seed plants grow in different places.
1. They may grow in cold or hot places.
2. They may grow in sunlight or shade.
3. They may grow in very wet or very dry places.
4. Some seed plants even grow in water.
5. Seed plants grow in open fields, gardens, cracks of sidewalks, and flowerpots.

Textbook Application
Finding Topic, Main Idea, and Details in Science

A long article with many paragraphs can also have a topic, a main idea, and supporting details. Textbooks and other informational materials are often organized in this way. As you read these kinds of materials, look for the topic, the main idea, and the details. These will help you understand and remember what you are reading.

Read the paragraph below which is taken from a textbook. The sidenotes will help you find the topic, main idea, and details.

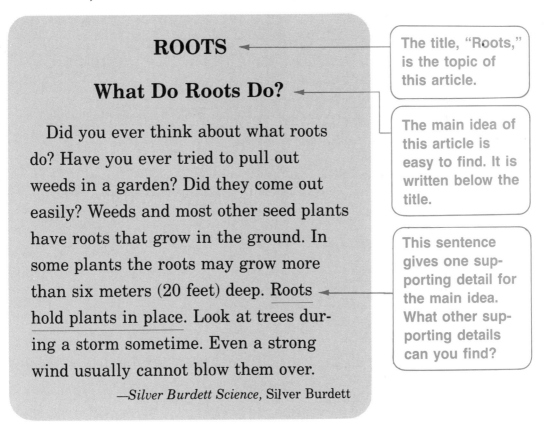

ROOTS

What Do Roots Do?

Did you ever think about what roots do? Have you ever tried to pull out weeds in a garden? Did they come out easily? Weeds and most other seed plants have roots that grow in the ground. In some plants the roots may grow more than six meters (20 feet) deep. Roots hold plants in place. Look at trees during a storm sometime. Even a strong wind usually cannot blow them over.

—*Silver Burdett Science*, Silver Burdett

The title, "Roots," is the topic of this article.

The main idea of this article is easy to find. It is written below the title.

This sentence gives one supporting detail for the main idea. What other supporting details can you find?

The sidenotes show the topic, the main idea, and the supporting details in the paragraph.

The topic is also the title of this paragraph. When a title is not given, you have to decide what the paragraph is about to find a topic.

Now read the paragraphs from another science book found on the next page. There is no title given. Decide what the topic and main idea are.

People are at work behind the glass walls. They are not in an office or a hospital. They are in a greenhouse. Green plants grow in the greenhouse.

These people know how plants grow. They pick the best seeds to grow the healthiest plants. They will sell some of the plants. They will use others to grow better plants. Some of the plants will have flowers with beautiful petals or flowers that smell sweet. Some will have better fruits and vegetables. Some will even have fruits without seeds.

—*HBJ Science,* Harcourt Brace Jovanovich

What is the topic? Since there is no title, you have to decide what the paragraphs are about. *Growing better plants* is the topic. What is the main idea? The main idea is not one of the sentences. The main idea is that people work in greenhouses to grow better plants.

What are the details that support the main idea?

1. The people know how plants grow.
2. They pick the best seeds.
3. They sell some plants.
4. They keep other plants to grow special flowers, vegetables, or fruit.

Now read these paragraphs taken from the same science book. Decide what the topic and main idea are.

> These are watermelon vines. They have many flowers. A bee may fly from flower to flower. When the flowers die the fruit begins to grow. Small watermelons grow where the flowers were.
>
> The watermelons grow larger. They get ripe. Inside each watermelon are seeds. If you plant the seeds you will get more vines. More vines make more fruit. Do you see why seeds are important?
>
> —*HBJ Science*, Harcourt Brace Jovanovich

What is the topic of the paragraphs? The topic is *watermelons*. What is the main idea of the paragraphs? The main idea is that seeds and flowers are important in producing watermelons. Can you find the supporting details for the main idea? Read the paragraphs again and look for the supporting details. Then, on a separate sheet of paper, write the supporting details in a list.

As you read textbooks, encyclopedias, or other informational materials, remember to look for the topic, main idea, and supporting details.

Beauty can be seen in nature. What are several ways that nature spreads its beauty?

Floaters, Poppers, and Parachutes

by Cynthia Overbeck Bix

Have you ever picked up a "wing" on the sidewalk under a maple tree and let it go spinning away on the wind? Or have you ever blown on a dandelion head and watched the white puffs float off like little parachutes? What about burrs? Have you ever picked one off your sock or some other piece of clothing?

If so, you have helped a seed find a new place to grow. The wing, the parachute, and the burr are parts of plants that carry seeds. Inside each seed are all the things needed to grow a new plant.

Wind Riders

From spring to autumn, the air and water are filled with these tiny travelers. Dry maple tree wings grow from small flowers. The flowers are on the maple tree in the spring. Each flower grows double wings with one seed in each wing. When the wings are ready to fall, they break apart and come spinning down from the tree. The wings have a good chance of being caught by the wind and carried away. If one of them lands in good soil, the seed inside it may sprout into a tree.

Dandelions also ride the wind. The yellow flower petals die and hundreds of tiny seeds are left on the white head of the dandelion. Each seed has silky hairs on top. When the wind catches these silky hairs, they float like little parachutes. When the silky hairs finally touch down, they may be far away from where they started. They leave their seeds in someone's yard, or in a field. The next spring, dandelions will be found growing where they had not grown before.

199

Floaters

Many wind travelers can also float on water because they are so light. The dandelion parachute or the maple wing may be carried by the wind and later be dropped into a stream.

Other travelers can move only by floating on water. The coconut has a hard shell as big as a football, with a large seed inside. It can float because it has lots of air spaces inside. When a ripe coconut falls from a tree onto the beach, the ocean currents may

200

carry it very far away. If the coconut is washed ashore on another beach, it may put down roots and grow into a coconut tree.

Many of the coconut trees that today line the beaches of the tropical Hawaiian Islands grew from coconuts that were washed ashore. The islands had no coconut trees or other plants when they were first formed. Most of the plants that now grow there were brought by water or wind from tropical beaches far away.

with many seeds is left. The ball is covered with very small spines. Each spine is bent at the end like a tiny fishhook and sticks to most things. When a passer-by brushes against a burdock plant, the hooks catch onto clothes or fur and stay there. The seeds fall out of the burr as it is carried along. Many of the seeds will take root in the ground, often far from the place where they were picked up.

Hitchhikers

Seeds fly and float. Some also hitchhike by catching free rides on the hair of dogs or wild animals, or on somebody's sock or pant leg. Many have hooks, barbs, or spines that stick to things.

One hitchhiking seed carrier that is easy to find is the burr. The burr comes from the burdock, a weed that grows almost any-where. When the burdock's flower dies, a dark-colored ball

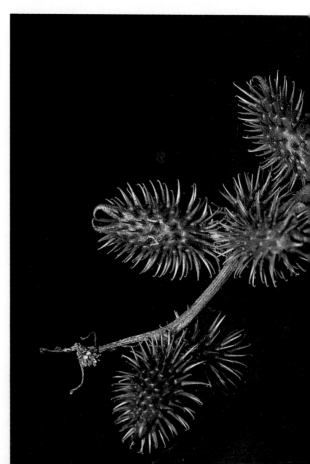

Poppers

Some seeds travel in a surprising way. They pop! The wild touch-me-not is a plant that spreads its seeds by popping. In the summer it has bright orange, yellow, or red flowers. Green pods grow from the flowers. Each pod has five parts with rows of seeds inside. When the pods have grown to their full length, the five parts suddenly curl up and pop. The seeds shoot out in many directions. They may travel as far as 2 yards, or 1.8 meters, away from the plant.

Flying, floating, hitchhiking, and popping seeds are always on the move. Many accidents may happen to them. They may be eaten by insects and animals. They may land on poor soil or on no soil at all. Still, enough seeds live for many new plants to grow.

The next time you take a walk, watch for the seeds of the many trees and plants around you. Once you begin to look, you will see the tiny travelers in the air, on the water — everywhere.

Discuss the Selection

1. How do seeds get to new places?

2. Why don't all seeds take root and grow?

3. Why do most seeds have wings, hairs, burrs, or pods?

4. Of all the ways that seeds travel, which do you think is the most interesting? Why?

5. When did you know why the author chose the title "Floaters, Poppers, and Parachutes"?

6. Why is this selection found in a unit called "Beauty"?

Think and Write

Prewrite

This story has given us a lot of information about seeds, which is the *topic* of the selection. Look back at the story with a classmate and notice how each paragraph gives more information about seeds. Also, notice how each paragraph has an idea all its own.

Like the author, you probably have a lot of information about something. It could be baseball, breakfast cereals, or your school. Think of something about which you have a lot of information.

Draft

Select a topic about which you have a lot of information and write several paragraphs on that topic. Make sure that each paragraph is about your main topic. Also, be sure that each paragraph has a central idea, an idea that is all its own.

Revise

Check over your work closely. Will it be clear to the reader what your topic is? Does each paragraph give more information? Does your first sentence make the reader want to know more? Revise your paragraphs to make them better.

Randolph Caldecott Medal Illustrator

Who is the Lupine Lady? What does she do to make the world more beautiful?

Miss Rumphius

story and pictures by Barbara Cooney

The Lupine Lady lives in a small house overlooking the sea. In between the rocks around her house grow blue and purple and rose-colored flowers. The Lupine Lady is little and old, but she has not always been that way. I know. She is my great-aunt, and she told me so.

Once upon a time there was a little girl, named Alice, who lived in a city by the sea. From the front steps she could see the masts of tall ships. Many years ago her grandfather had come to America on a large sailing ship. Now he lived in the shop at the bottom of the house making figureheads for the front-ends of ships. He also painted pictures of sailing ships and places across the sea. When he was very busy, Alice helped him by painting the skies.

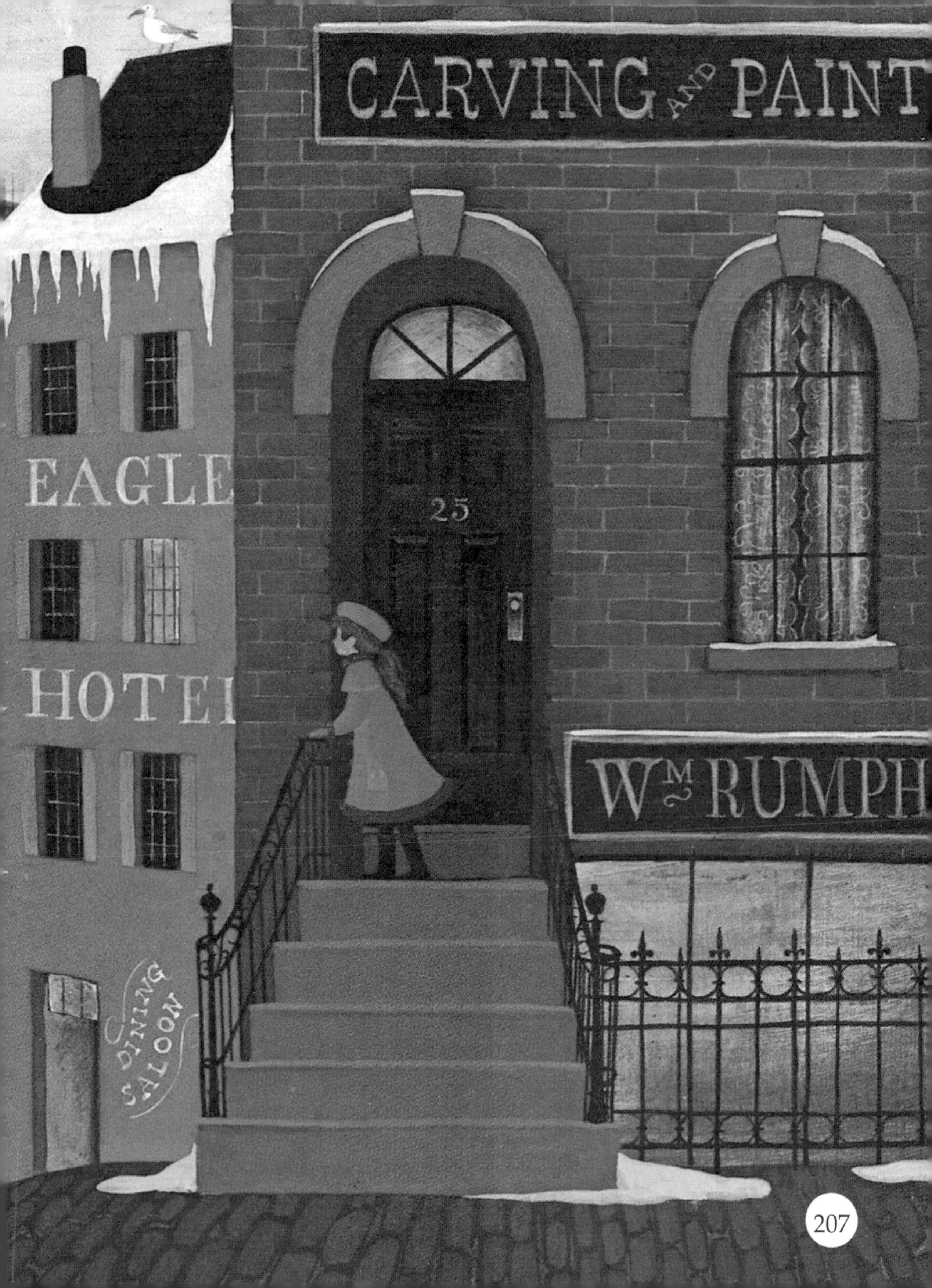
CARVING AND PAINT
EAGLE
HOTEL
25
Wm RUMPH
DINING SALOON

In the evening Alice sat on her grandfather's knee and listened to his stories of faraway places. When he had finished, Alice would say, "When I grow up, I too will go to faraway places, and when I grow old, I too will live beside the sea."

"That is all very well, little Alice," said her grandfather, "but there is a third thing you must do."

"What is that?" asked Alice.

"You must do something to make the world more beautiful," said her grandfather.

"All right," said Alice. But she did not know what that could be.

In the meantime Alice got up and washed her face and ate breakfast. She went to school and came home and did her homework.

And pretty soon she was grown up.

Then my Great-aunt Alice set out to do the three things she had told her grandfather she was going to do. She left home and went to live in another city far from the sea and the salt air. There she worked in a library, dusting books and keeping them from getting mixed up and helping people find the ones they wanted. Some of the books told her about faraway places.

People called her Miss Rumphius now.

Sometimes she went to the conservatory in the middle of the park. When she stepped inside on a wintry day, the warm air wrapped itself around her, and the sweet smell of the flowers filled her nose. "This is almost like a tropical island," said Miss Rumphius. "But not quite."

So Miss Rumphius went to a real tropical island, where people kept monkeys as pets. She walked on long beaches, picking up beautiful shells.

My great-aunt Miss Alice Rumphius climbed tall mountains where the snow never melted. She went through jungles and across deserts. Finally she came to another island, and there, getting off a camel, she hurt her back.

"Well," said Miss Rumphius, "I have certainly seen faraway places. Maybe it is time to find my place by the sea."

And it was, and she did.

From the porch of her new house Miss Rumphius
watched the sun come up; she watched it cross the sky
and sparkle on the water; and she saw it set in glory in
the evening. She started a little garden among the rocks
that surrounded her house, and she planted a few flower
seeds in the stony ground. Miss Rumphius was *almost*
perfectly happy.

"But there is still one more thing I have to do," she
said. "I have to do something to make the world more
beautiful.

"But what? The world already is pretty nice," she
thought, looking out at the ocean.

The next spring Miss Rumphius was not very well. Her back was bothering her again, and she had to stay in bed most of the time.

The flowers she had planted the summer before had come up and bloomed in spite of the stony ground. She could see them from her bedroom window, blue and purple and rose-colored.

"Lupines," said Miss Rumphius with satisfaction. "I have always loved lupines the best. I wish I could plant more seeds this summer so that I could have still more flowers next year."

She was not able to.

After a hard winter spring came. Miss Rumphius was feeling much better. Now she could take walks again. One afternoon she started to go up and over the hill, where she had not been in a long time.

"I don't believe my eyes!" she cried when she got to the top. For there on the other side of the hill was a large patch of blue and purple and rose-colored lupines!

"It was the wind," she said as she knelt in delight. "It was the wind that brought the seeds from my garden here! And the birds must have helped!"

She hurried home and got out her seed catalogues. She sent off to the very best seed house for five bushels of lupine seed.

All that summer Miss Rumphius, her pockets full of seeds, wandered over fields and headlands, sowing lupines. She scattered seeds along the highways and down the country lanes. She flung handfuls of seeds around the schoolhouse and back of the church. She tossed them into hollows and along stone walls.

Her back didn't bother her anymore at all.

The next spring there were lupines everywhere. Fields and hillsides were covered with blue and purple and rose-colored flowers. They bloomed along the highways and down the lanes. Bright patches lay around the schoolhouse and back of the church. Down in the hollows and along the stone walls grew the beautiful flowers.

Miss Rumphius had done the third, the most difficult thing of all!

My Great-aunt Alice, Miss Rumphius, is very old now. Her hair is very white. Every year there are more and more lupines. Now they call her the Lupine Lady. Sometimes my friends stand with me outside her gate, curious to see the old, old lady who planted the fields of lupines. When she invites them in, they come slowly. They think she is the oldest woman in the world. Often she tells us stories of faraway places.

"When I grow up," I tell her, "I too will go to faraway places and come home to live by the sea."

"That is all very well, little Alice," says my great-aunt, "but there is a third thing you must do."

"What is that?" I ask.

"You must do something to make the world more beautiful."

"All right," I say.

But I do not know yet

       what that can be.

1. How did the Lupine Lady get her name?

2. What were the three things Miss Rumphius wanted to do during her life?

3. How did Miss Rumphius keep her promise to her grandfather?

4. Do you think little Alice will be able to keep her promise to her great-aunt? Why?

5. When did you know what the Lupine Lady did to make the world more beautiful?

6. All of us in our own way can make the world more beautiful. What idea does Miss Rumphius give you about adding beauty to the world?

Prewrite

In the story, the third thing Alice's grandfather told her she must do was to "do something to make the world more beautiful." If you were given that order, what would you like to do to make the world more beautiful? Think about how you would do it.

Draft

Choose one of the activities below:

1. Pretend that you have been given the job of making the world more beautiful. Write a story about what you would like to do to accomplish your task. How would it make the world more beautiful?

2. Write a story about something that the whole class could really do to make the world more beautiful. How could it be done and how would it make the world more beautiful?

Revise

Read your story to yourself, and then to a classmate. Does it seem convincing that your task would make the world more beautiful? Discuss some possible changes with a classmate and then revise your story.

Artists add beauty to the world in many ways. How does one popular author and illustrator share beauty with others?

Interview with Barbara Cooney

adapted from an article by Julia Smith

Barbara Cooney is an award-winning author and illustrator of picture books for children. She won the 1983 American Book Award for *Miss Rumphius*.

Barbara Cooney has also won two Caldecott Awards. The Caldecott Award is given each year for the best illustrations in a children's book.

As you read the following interview, you will feel as if you are talking directly to Barbara Cooney. You will learn why this creative author and illustrator decided to work on children's books and what she is like as a person.

Question: Why did you decide to become an illustrator of children's books?

Answer: When I was young, I loved reading series books. They went on and on and you didn't have to say good-bye to the characters. Of course I read other books, too—all the time. Books help you create pictures in your mind.

My mother was an artist who loved to paint. She helped me experiment with color. After I finished school, I knew I wanted to paint pictures. I decided that illustrating books for children would let me be the most creative.

Question: Where did you get the idea to write and illustrate *Miss Rumphius*?

Answer: My husband and I were building a house in Maine. I asked one of the painters why there were so many lovely flowers growing all around. He told me about Hilda. Hilda is a real-life Lupine Lady who planted the lupines. The story began to grow in my mind, until one day, I sat down and wrote it. I had something in my head and I just had to get it out. *Miss Rumphius* was the result.

Question: Did you put anything from your own life in the illustrations for *Miss Rumphius*?

Answer: I put in lots of little details that make me happy. These are my shawl, my favorite armchair, and a picture of my grandson. I don't know if other people notice all these details, but they make me happy.

Question: You have won two Caldecott Awards for your illustrations. What books received those awards?

Answer: I won the Caldecott Award in 1959 for the illustrations in *Chanticleer and the Fox.* Many of my early illustrations were of animals. People will give you little furry animal stories if you draw good fur.

Then, in 1980, I won a second Caldecott Award for *Ox-Cart Man*. I spent most of my life in New England. That is why I was able to show a farmer and his family and the busy marketplace in that book.

Question: How do you begin to illustrate a book?

Answer: When I begin to illustrate a book, I start with page one. Books are like movies. One's eye moves from frame to frame in a sequence. I must keep that sequence in mind to keep the reader's eye always interested.

First, I make what is called a dummy of the book. It is a rough, messy copy of what the book will be like. Then, I begin the final illustrations, working carefully to get just the right colors, and just the perfect tone. The book jacket comes last. The book jacket is like the label on a can of tomatoes. You can't put a tomato on the label until you know you have a tomato in the can.

Question: What other things do you like to do besides work on children's books?

Answer: I also love to garden, cook, photograph, travel the world, and be a grandmother. I love life and plan to live to be one hundred years old!

219

1. How does the interview with Barbara Cooney tell about the way she shares beauty with others?

2. Why did Barbara Cooney become a children's book illustrator?

3. What awards have Barbara Cooney's books received?

4. Why do you think an interview with Barbara Cooney is included in this book?

5. How does the interview help you learn what Barbara Cooney is like as a person?

6. Barbara Cooney's works are beautiful to look at. How do you think the stories she writes also add beauty to the world?

Prewrite

Think about a person in your school or a person in your town whom you would like to interview. Think about what you already know about this person. What questions would you like to ask this person?

Draft

Write an introduction about the person you would like to interview, similar to the introduction on the first page of this selection. Next, write a list of eight questions you would like to ask this person. They should be questions that would help a reader or listener know more about the person.

Revise

Look over your questions and share them with a classmate. See if he or she has any additional questions for your person. Add his or her questions to your list.

Thinking About "Beauty"

Beauty is all around you. Like the world of the Wizard, our world is full of color. There is beauty in a blazing sunset or on a hillside that Miss Rumphius helped cover with colorful lupines. Music can be beautiful, too. It can be a song you heard or the music Andro made for Ty and his friends.

In this unit you learned that people look for beauty in different things. What did the Queen learn about the real meaning of beauty? How does Barbara Cooney express her ideas about beauty to her readers? How have the stories taught you that beauty can be found almost everywhere if you look and listen carefully?

The way you look at something helps you decide whether or not it is beautiful. As you read other stories, decide how the characters are helping you find new ways to see beauty.

1. Which characters in this unit made the world a more beautiful place? How did each character do that?

2. How are the Wizard and Miss Rumphius alike? How are they different?

3. How are Barbara Cooney and Andro alike? Explain how they are different.

4. How is the Queen's way of looking at beauty different from the Wizard's way of looking at beauty?

5. Which of the stories you read in this unit expresses your own idea of beauty? Explain your answer.

Unit 4

Milestones

Long ago, when there were no road signs, large stones were put by the side of the road to mark the miles. That is how the word *milestone* came to be. Today, a milestone has come to mean any important time or turning point in a person's life.

Something challenging happens to the characters in "Milestones." Imagine what it would be like to have journeyed into the wilderness long ago. How might it feel to be different from everyone in school? What would it be like to do what no one else has ever done?

As you read the selections in this unit, you will discover how some of the characters have made a lasting mark on the world in which we live. How do you think the milestones they reach have changed their lives?

225

Ride the Red Cycle *by Harriette Gillem Robinet. Houghton.* Jerome dreams of riding a cycle, but he can't walk and has other problems. With courage and help, he learns to ride. He isn't always nice or happy, but he is always brave.

Sybil Rides for Independence *by Drollene P. Brown. Whitman.* A young girl in Connecticut wants to help the American fight for independence. She makes a difficult ride to warn the people of danger.

From Path to Highway: The Story of the Boston Post Road *by Gail Gibbons. Crowell.* Five hundred years ago, Indians walked the paths we now travel by car. This book tells all about this interesting fact.

My Village, Sturbridge *by Gary Bowen. Farrar.* This book tells what it was like to live in a New England village in the early 1800's.

Ramona and Her Father *by Beverly Cleary. Morrow.* Ramona's family has to make some changes when her father loses his job.

How Far, Filipe? *by Genevieve Gray. Harper.* Filipe and his donkey endure many hardships with their group as they travel from Mexico to settle in California.

Encyclopedia Brown Shows the Way *by Donald J. Sobol. Bantam.* A boy detective solves ten crimes in this book. The solutions to the crimes are at the end of the book.

Mrs. Dunphy's Dog *by Catherine O'Neill. Viking.* James, the amazing dog, learns to read the newspaper, and what he reads astounds him. This dog can even read books!

The Flunking of Joshua T. Bates *by Susan Shreve. Knopf.* Repeat third grade? Joshua would rather leave home! At first it is worse than he thought it would be, but a good teacher becomes his friend, and things turn out for the best.

John Newbery Medal Author

What is Uncle Joseph's plan? What makes this plan so unusual?

Away Goes Sally

by Elizabeth Coatsworth

Sally lived in Old New England with three aunts and two uncles. The family was made up of Aunt Nannie, Aunt Deborah, Aunt Esther, Uncle Joseph, Uncle Eben, and Sally.

After Uncle Joseph received a letter from his cousin in Maine, Uncle Joseph was ready to move the family. He wanted to go to Maine because there were few settlers there. Everyone wanted to move, too, except for his sister Nannie. Aunt Nannie wanted to stay in Massachusetts where they had a nice house and farm. Aunt Nannie told her family that she would never leave her own fire nor sleep in any bed but her own. Uncle Joseph thought of a way to change Aunt Nannie's mind.

As the story begins, Sally and her aunts are returning from a visit to the city of Quincy.

228

They drove home quickly. When Dorcas, the mare, stopped at the back door it was still light. There was no sign of the uncles or of their hired hand, Jehoshaphat Mountain. Sally started to take the mare to the barn. She was stopped by several voices coming down the road. She heard men's voices, and the screech of heavy runners on snow. The three aunts paused on the doorstep. Sally jumped from the sleigh to watch. Out of the darkness of the last pine trees appeared the strangest thing she had ever seen.

First came Peacock, Uncle Joseph's big horse, with Uncle Joseph on his back. Then came six strong oxen, led by the red pair from their own farm. Beside them

walked Jehoshaphat Mountain and Uncle Eben with long poles. Behind them came a little house on runners. It was a house with windows whose small panes sparkled in the late light. The house had a doorstep, a water-barrel under the drip of the roof, and a chimney pipe from which smoke was rising.

Sally jumped up and down, clapping her mittened hands. Aunt Esther cried in delight. Uncle Joseph waved. Aunt Nannie made no sound.

Slowly the line drew to the step and stopped.

"Nannie," said Uncle Joseph in a serious voice, "here is a house that I built for you and which I give to you with all my heart. Now you may travel to Maine and yet never leave your own fire."

He paused and they all waited. Aunt Nannie's face was blank with surprise and did not show her thoughts. Once she tried to speak but could not. In the long silence Sally heard her own heart pounding like a colt galloping over a frozen meadow.

"Thank you, Brother Joseph," said Aunt Nannie at last in a small gentle voice. "Thank you, my dear. I shall go willingly."

Sally let her breath out in a gasp of joy. Uncle Joseph jumped from the saddle and kissed Aunt Nannie, who cried a little.

"Dorcas will take herself to the barn, Sally," Uncle Joseph called. "Come and see Aunt Nannie's house." They all crowded into the house.

The house was small, of course, but bright with windows. It was warm with the Franklin stove which had a little fire burning in it. Two big beds stood in two corners of the room. They were covered with blue eagle woven quilts. There was a smooth wooden sink and several chairs, and china in racks on the walls. Behind the larger room was a small room with two bunks in it for the uncles.

"There will be sleds for the rest of the furniture, Nannie," went on Uncle Joseph. "I have hired some men and their teams from down the road. You will, I imagine, wish to take our cows. Dorcas and the sleigh will bring up the rear, so that you may all get some air when you grow tired of being in the house. Here, Deborah, are your seeds for a new garden. We will carry some of your bulbs and roots on the sleds."

"How soon do we leave, Brother Joseph?" Aunt Nannie asked as she hung up her cloak on a peg and seated herself in her own chair.

"It's a picture to see you," said Uncle Joseph, smiling at her. They looked at each other and made their peace without a word being spoken. "I wanted this to be a surprise for you like the doll's house I made when you were a little girl. That's why I packed you all off to Quincy

to have you out of the way while we furnished the house. You asked when we would leave, Nannie. In a week, if you can be ready, my dear, so that we may have the advantage of the snow. The neighbors will help you."

"It will be a long trip," went on Uncle Joseph. "When we reach our land, we shall have this house to live in until we can build a better new home, Nannie, on a wider piece of land."

It was Sally who discovered the six little pots steaming in the rack on the stove. Uncle Eben, always ready to help in any matter of food, showed Sally where a pine table let down from the wall. She found the cloth and silver spoons and the bread. Soon six cups were filled, and they shared their first meal in the house that was to carry them to a new land.

1. What was Uncle Joseph's plan?

2. Why was Uncle Joseph's plan so unusual?

3. Why do you think Aunt Nannie agreed to move?

4. Do you think Uncle Joseph's plan was a good idea? Explain your answer.

5. When did you know that Aunt Nannie would not have to leave her fire?

6. How did Uncle Joseph prove that where there's a will, there's a way?

Think and Write

Prewrite

In the story, Aunt Nannie did not want to leave behind her own fire and bed to move to Maine with her family. Think about what it would be like to move. With a classmate, discuss and then list the things that you would most want to take with you. What are the things that are very important to you? Why are they important? The following chart will help you to think about these questions.

What to Take	Why

Draft

Write a paragraph about the things that you feel you would have to take with you if you moved. Choose three or four things that are important to you personally. Explain why each of these things is important and why you feel you would need to take each with you. Refer to your list as you write.

Revise

Check your paragraph.Have you explained why each item is imortant to you? Let a classmate read your paragraph and then list the items you said were important. Ask your classmate to tell why they were important. If he or she cannot remember, revise your paragraph to make it very clear.

Maps

Mr. Brown's third-grade class took a trip to Old Sturbridge Village. When they got to the village, Mr. Brown stopped at the Visitor Center to pick up a map to help the group find its way around the village. On the next page is the map they used.

Look at the map on page 237. It shows all of Old Sturbridge Village and has labels for the four sections. Notice that there is a small map placed in the corner of the large map. This small map is called an **inset map.** An inset map takes one portion of a map and enlarges that part to show more details. On this map of Old Sturbridge Village, the inset is showing, in detail, the section called Center Village. It shows and labels the houses and buildings found there.

Use the map of Old Sturbridge Village and the inset map of Center Village to answer the questions.

1. What building is between Thompson Bank and Fenno House?
2. What building is next to the Gebhardt Barn?
3. What building is between Salem Towne House and Fitch House?

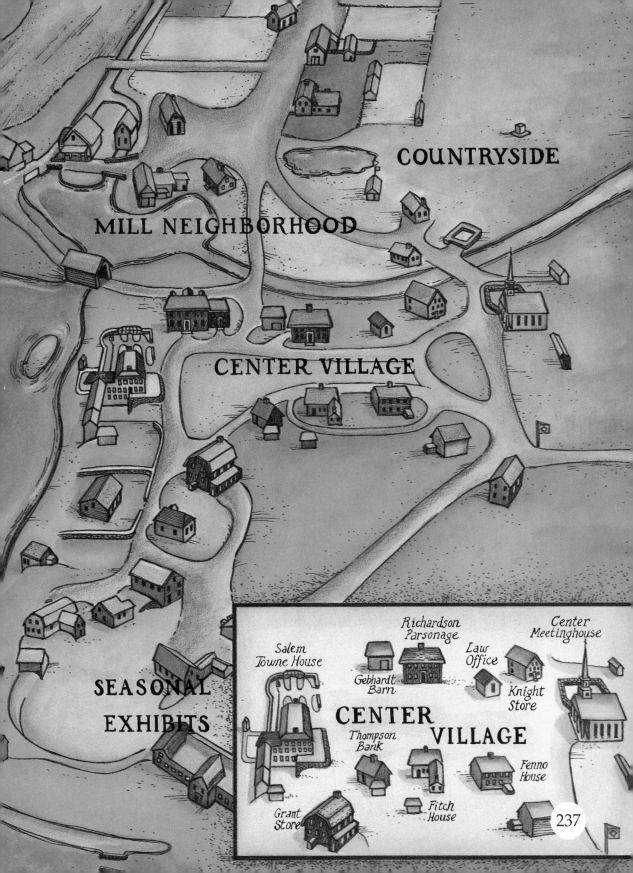

COUNTRYSIDE

MILL NEIGHBORHOOD

CENTER VILLAGE

SEASONAL EXHIBITS

Salem Towne House

Richardson Parsonage

Gebhardt Barn

Law Office

Center Meetinghouse

Knight Store

CENTER VILLAGE

Thompson Bank

Fenno House

Grant Store

Fitch House

237

Albert Wells had an idea for an unusual museum. Read to find out what life is like at a living history museum.

A Visit to Old Sturbridge Village

by Peter Roop

An Unusual Museum

Albert Wells liked to collect old tools and household items. He had old chairs, jugs, dishes, hammers, and saws. He kept these things because they helped him better understand and feel closer to the people who lived long ago.

Albert Wells collected so many things that he had to build a special room onto his house. He added more and more things to his collection. Then he put two barns together to hold everything, but the barns were soon filled. Finally, his family had to move out of their home to make more room.

Albert Wells decided to build a museum for his collection. Mr. Wells thought about creating a museum that would be a place where visitors could see farms and homes just as they were 150 years ago. It would be run by people living and working just as the people did in the early days of America.

238

Albert Wells and his brother, Cheney, bought land along a river in Massachusetts for their village. They searched New England for old churches, houses, shops, and barns. Then they bought the buildings and moved them to their village. Slowly, over many years, more than 40 buildings were brought to the village.

Albert Wells called this unusual museum a living history museum. He created a place where visitors could experience what everyday life was like in a New England village between 1790 and 1840.

The living history village was named Old Sturbridge Village. In 1946, Old Sturbridge Village was opened. Today over 500,000 people visit this unusual living village each year.

A Trip Back in Time

A visit to Old Sturbridge Village is like stepping back into the days before there was electricity or cars or engines for machines. Imagine what our world would be like without televisions, refrigerators, airplanes, and trucks.

A visitor at Old Sturbridge Village will notice that it is divided into four sections: the Center Village, the Countryside, the Mill Neighborhood, and the Seasonal Exhibits. Each section offers something different to see.

The Center Village

The Center Village has homes in which people live, a working printing office, a bank, a general store, a law office, and two meeting houses. These buildings have been placed around an open green space called the Common. The Center Village looks the way a real village would have looked between 1790 and 1840.

At that time, hundreds of small farms usually surrounded a village. The farm families came to town to trade or buy things that they needed. They also came to meet friends and relatives or to attend church meetings.

Visitors to the Printing Office watch a printer "ink and draw" pages for a book. They see the printer's helper hang pages to dry like clothes on a line.

The Countryside

The Pliny Freeman Farm is found in the Countryside. This is a real working farm. The farmhouse is like those built in the 1800's, furnished with tables, chairs, and beds.

The people living at the Pliny Freeman Farm do all of the

The Mill Neighborhood

chores. The cows are milked by hand, and the cream is hand churned to make butter. The food is cooked over an open fire in a kitchen. Wool from the farm's sheep is made into cloth for clothes. A vegetable garden is planted and carefully tended. A team of trained oxen is used to do the heavy work.

The Mill Neighborhood is a very important part of the village. Most New England towns had mills powered by water. Old Sturbridge Village has three working mills.

The farmers use the Grist Mill to grind grain to make flour. The Carding Mill is used to comb, smooth, and straighten wool. The wool is then made ready for spinning into yarn. At the Sawmill heavy logs are cut into boards for houses, barns, and other buildings. This is much faster and easier than cutting boards by hand.

The Seasonal Exhibits

The displays in the Seasonal Exhibit Area change depending on the season of the year. In the winter months visitors see how wool is spun to make cloth. During the warmer months they see how breads are baked in the Bake-House. There are displays around an herb garden where many of the plants used for seasoning foods are grown.

A Living Village

Every New England village needed people with special skills. These skills were barrel-making, shoemaking, pottery making, and blacksmithing. Old Sturbridge Village has people doing these jobs so that visitors can see just how these jobs were done.

Scattered throughout Old Sturbridge Village are shops and offices of the craftsmen and tradesmen. In the Potter's Shop visitors watch a potter take the clay he dug out of the ground and spin and shape it into a bowl. Then he hardens it in his special oven. At the Cooper Shop visitors see how buckets and barrels are made. The clanging of the blacksmith's hammer is loud as he repairs broken tools. He also makes horseshoes and tools.

The District School at Old Sturbridge Village is a one-room school just like a school in early America. Then, children of all ages from 5 to 14 sat

together on hard wooden benches in one room. There they learned to read, write, and count. In the District School, students write on tablets and recite lessons for their teacher.

It is hard work to make so many things at Old Sturbridge Village just like those of long ago. Those who live there enjoy living like their ancestors. They enjoy making history come alive.

History comes alive, too, for the many people who visit Old Sturbridge Village every year. They have a chance to step back in time for a day. They can find out what life was like when America was a young country. This is just what Albert Wells had in mind.

1. What makes Old Sturbridge Village seem real to visitors?

2. What do visitors learn at Old Sturbridge Village?

3. How was Old Sturbridge Village built?

4. If you went to Old Sturbridge Village, what do you think you would like best?

5. How does the author let you know that Old Sturbridge Village is a place to learn about early village life?

6. How do you think this living history museum makes a lasting mark on those who visit it?

Prewrite

You have read an informational article about Old Sturbridge Village. An article like this gives you new information and facts. Look over the article and think about some of the things you learned about Old Sturbridge Village. Think about what it would have been like to live in

244

such a village 150 years ago. How was life then different from your life today? Use the following chart to help you compare life then and now.

	Then	Now
Food	▬▬▬▬▬	▬▬▬▬
Clothes	▬▬▬▬	▬▬▬▬
Transportation	▬▬▬▬	▬▬▬▬
Entertainment	▬▬▬▬	▬▬▬▬

Draft

Write a story that compares life in Sturbridge Village 150 years ago to your life today. How would life for a child have been different 150 years ago from what it is now?

Revise

Look over your story and the story in the book. Are there more details you could add to your story to improve it? Are all your facts correct? Add to your story or correct it to make it the best you can do!

Textbook Application:
Outlining in Social Studies

Read this article from a textbook. Use the side-notes to find the topic and main idea.

This title tells you the topic of the article.

This heading tells you the first main idea.

This heading is the second main idea.

COMMUNITY SERVICES

Transportation Services

Do you take a city bus to school? If so, you are using public transportation. Buses and trains are two kinds of public transportation. They are another kind of service many communities provide to people. People pay money when they ride public transportation.

Health Services

Many communities have hospitals to care for people who are hurt or sick. Most hospitals have emergency rooms. People can get help right away at a hospital emergency room.

Community clinics are also places that treat people who are hurt or ill. At many clinics there are doctors and dentists who can take care of the whole family.

Public Schools

What is this heading?

One community service you know about is the public school system. Most communities have a board of education. Its members are elected by the people of the community.

In many communities, it is up to the board of education to help choose teachers. The board decides how the schools should be run. The board does an important job. A good education gives people a good start in life.

—*Communities*, Harcourt Brace Jovanovich

An outline of the article would look like this:

Community Services
    I. Transportation Services
    II. Health Services
    III. Public Schools

The main ideas in an outline give the most important points. After you have read, review the important ideas that the author has provided. By putting these ideas in an outline, you will be able to remember the most important points of what you have just read.

Who is Cri-Cri?[1] Why is he famous in Mexico today?

Cri-Cri, The Singing Cricket

by Carmen García Moreno

Cri-Cri, the Singing Cricket, is the best-known and the most-loved character of Mexican children. Thousands of Mexican children have listened to his songs and stories. The little country cricket likes to sing and play the violin and is wise and funny.

---

[1] Cri-Cri [crē'-crē]

250

Francisco Gabilondo Soler[2] is the man who gave life to Cri-Cri. Francisco is as unforgettable as the character he created. He was born in 1907 in Orizaba,[3] which is in the state of Veracruz[4] in Mexico.

Francisco had a happy childhood. He was especially close to his grandmother and loved to listen to the stories she told him. These are the same stories and songs which have given joy and happiness to thousands of children.

As a child Francisco loved to run to the open country, not far away from his home, and sit for hours. He liked to look at the clouds, the flowers, the animals, and the sunsets. He wondered about

---

[2] Francisco Gabilondo Soler [fran•sēs′kō gab′ē•lon′dō sō•lär′]
[3] Orizaba [or′ē•za′bə]
[4] Veracruz [ver′ə•krōōz′]

Most of the songs have been recorded and the records are still popular today. Each song is really a funny story with a message or meaning. Like any good story, each song touches the imagination and sense of adventure of its listeners.

Francisco said that every time he remembered his childhood he wrote down a funny story so others could enjoy all the wonderful tales of his everyday life. He said that writing the stories and songs has given him such great pleasure that he would not trade that for anything in the world.

Francisco turned 80 years old in 1987. He celebrated 50 years of telling his tales and sharing his songs on Mexican radio. He has lived a long and full life. He is retired now and spends most of his time in his home where he still studies astronomy and reads. Though Francisco no longer records new songs, Cri-Cri's music is still heard on the radio.

As everybody knows, crickets like to hide. Cri-Cri still hides behind the radio. He does not need the movie or television screen. Children can imagine him and his adventures. When the sun sets, his songs can be heard coming from the radio or from a record, wherever there are Mexican children.

1. Who is Cri-Cri? Why is Cri-Cri so well-known in Mexico?

2. What other jobs has Francisco Gabilondo Soler had?

3. How did Francisco's work as a song and story writer help him to accomplish other things in life?

4. How do you think having so many different jobs changed Francisco's life?

5. When did you first begin to know that as a young boy Francisco had the qualities of a writer?

6. Why are the things Francisco accomplished considered milestones?

Prewrite

Francisco liked to tell the stories of his childhood. Think of some of the best times you had when you were younger. Make a list of some of the things that have happened to you. Share your list with a classmate and choose one experience about which to write.

Draft

Write a story of one of your favorite experiences. Be sure to start at the beginning and tell the whole story, including why it was a happy time for you.

Revise

Look over your story carefully. Does it have a good beginning and a good ending? Have you given enough details and information about your experience to make it interesting for the reader? Make the changes necessary to improve your story.

It Couldn't Be Done

by Edgar A. Guest

Somebody said that it couldn't be done,
   But he with a chuckle replied
That "maybe it couldn't," but he would be one
   Who wouldn't say so till he'd tried.
So he buckled right in with the trace of a grin
   On his face. If he worried he hid it.
He started to sing as he tackled the thing
   That couldn't be done, and he did it.

What mystery does Maggie solve? What lesson does the pirate learn?

Randolph Caldecott Medal Illustrator

Maggie and the Pirate

*story and pictures
by Ezra Jack Keats*

Maggie was feeding Niki, her pet cricket, when her mother called from across the river.

"Maggie! Come over please! I need some things from the grocery."

"Okay, Ma, we'll be right there."

Maggie paddled home.

Maggie hung Niki's cage on a tree next to her house. Then she got her mother's shopping list, and was off.

"Bye, bye, Niki. Have a nice snooze," she called.

On her way she passed her friends.

"Hey, what a cage my Pop built for Niki!" she yelled.

"Wow! Are you lucky!" called Paco. "Can we see it?"

"Sure—I'll pick you up on my way home," said Maggie.

On her way back she picked up Paco and Katie. They helped her carry the groceries home. When they got to the tree, something was missing! The cage and Niki were gone!

Instead there was a note.

"Pirate?" asked Katie.

"Yeah, who's the pirate?" Paco asked.

Maggie stared at the note in horror.

Paco and Katie tried and tried to take her mind
off Niki. It was no use.

"I miss Niki," Maggie sighed, "and that pirate—
he won't know what to feed him—Niki might
starve."

Maggie began tacking up signs.

"What's so special about a cricket anyway?" asked
Katie.

"I like him—that's what! I'm going to find that
pirate!" shouted Maggie.

"We'll come, too," said Paco.

"How will we know what he looks like?"

"What if he's bigger than us?" whispered Katie.
They started out.

They looked and looked. They couldn't find the
pirate anywhere. Her friends got tired and straggled behind.

Maggie stopped and listened. Crickets were chirp-
ing in the night.

"I must find Niki—before it's too late!" she said.

Suddenly, she came upon a tree house she'd never seen before. She walked over softly, climbed up very quietly, and peeped in.

IT WAS THE PIRATE'S HIDEOUT!

There was the pirate holding Niki's cage!

"Hey—I know you—and that's my cricket!"

Maggie dived into the tree house. She scuffled with the pirate, trying with all her strength to get Niki.

SPLASH!

The tree house came loose and crashed into the water!

Maggie sloshed around in the dark, searching for Niki. She saw something familiar floating by. It was the cage! She fished it out, and opened it. There was Niki! He didn't move.

"Niki's dead! He drowned," Maggie cried.

She ran off with Niki, leaving the cage behind.

"Maggie," she heard her friends call.

She saw Paco and Katie.

They ran to her. "Wow! Look at you! What happened? Did you find Niki?" asked Katie.

Maggie opened her hand and showed them.

"Poor Niki," said Paco.

Maggie told them everything that had happened.

"... and the pirate is that new kid around here," she said.

"So he's the one," whispered Katie.

They buried Niki.

Maggie wrote his name on a piece of wood and put it over the small grave. Paco picked some flowers and brought them over. Then they sang sad songs.

Suddenly, the pirate appeared!

"Why did you do that?" asked Maggie. "We never did anything to you!"

"It was the cage—I wanted it real bad," said the pirate. "I didn't mean for the cricket to die. My dad—he never makes anything for me. He doesn't ever talk to me."

The pirate handed the cage to Maggie. She held it up. A beautiful sound came out! She looked in. There was a new cricket inside.

They all sat down together. Nobody said anything. They listened to the new cricket singing. Crickets all around joined in.

1. What mystery does Maggie solve?

2. Why did the pirate steal the cage?

3. How did you feel when Maggie found the dead cricket?

4. How did the pirate try to make Maggie feel better?

5. When did you know that Maggie had solved the mystery?

6. What lesson did the pirate learn?

Think and Write

Prewrite

Maggie really liked the cage her dad made for her cricket. Think about something special that belongs to you. Why is it special? Where did you get it? How long have you had it? Copy the following web onto a piece of paper. Complete the web with information about your special treasure. Write some words that describe it in the small circles.

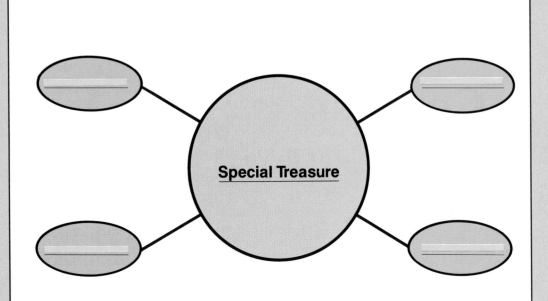

Special Treasure

Draft

Write a paragraph about your special treasure. Tell what it is, where you got it, and why it is special to you. Use the completed web for help. Include plenty of details in your paragraph.

Revise

Read your paragraph over and make sure it describes your special treasure. Add more details if they are needed.

Going to a new school causes special problems for Mike. Who helps Mike solve some of these problems? How?

A Contest

by Sherry Neuwirth Payne

Mike is ten. He's in fifth grade. He used to go to a special school where all his friends had crutches or wheelchairs like his. He and his friends did a lot of fun things in their wheelchairs. Sometimes they had races in their wheelchairs. Mike likes races and games.

What Mike doesn't like is people who stare at him. Mike's legs don't work. He wears braces on his legs. Since Mike can't use his legs, he will always need a wheelchair.

Now Mike is at a new school. Here Mike needs help with some things. The cartons of milk in the cafeteria are too far away for Mike to reach without spilling the tray in his lap. Mike also needs help with all the doors. At first he was afraid to ask anyone for help. Everyone seemed to stare at him.

On the first day of school a boy named Randy grabbed Mike's orange baseball hat and ran away with it. Mike hated his new school.

When Mike told his dad about it, his dad said, "It's not easy, is it, Mike? You have to live with all kinds of people. A good place to start learning about them is in school." Mike said he'd still go, but he wouldn't like it.

Mike's teacher, Mrs. Kocher, must have noticed his sad face, because one day she asked Mike to stay after school.

"Mike," she said, "you don't like this school very much, do you?"

"I sure don't, Mrs. Kocher," Mike said. "I'm the only kid in a wheelchair. I feel so different."

"I'll bet you do," Mrs. Kocher said. "What we need to do is show the other kids the ways you're not so different. I have an idea. What can you do especially well?"

"Well, I'm really good at checkers," said Mike. "I play with my father almost every day, and I'm good at arm wrestling."

"Arm wrestling?" said Mrs. Kocher. "That might be just the thing. We could have a contest. There are some pretty strong kids in this class, especially Randy."

"I'm sure I could win if you'd just give me a chance," Mike said.

"Why don't you try me first," said Mrs. Kocher. "See if you can beat me."

It didn't take long for Mike to push Mrs. Kocher's arm to the table. Mrs. Kocher looked a little surprised. Then she winked at Mike. "Arm wrestling it is then," she said with a smile.

The next day when all the children were at their desks, Mrs. Kocher asked, "Who would like to have an arm-wrestling contest today?" Every hand in the room shot up.

"Good. Susan and Mary, would you like to start?" Susan and Mary sat at the table facing each other.

They put their elbows on the table and locked hands. "One, two, three, go!" Mrs. Kocher said.

Each person took a turn with the winner. Randy won his first match easily. He won every match after that, too. Finally everyone had taken a turn and Randy was still at the table.

"Now it's your turn, Mike. Would you like to try?" asked Mrs. Kocher.

"Arm wrestle him?" Randy said. "But I'll probably hurt him."

"Just try me," Mike said. He was nervous, but he smiled at Randy.

At first Randy looked as if he was afraid to touch Mike. Then they locked hands and put their elbows on the table. "One, two, three, go!" Mrs. Kocher said.

Then Mike pushed Randy's arm down to the table in a second. Randy looked surprised. "I just didn't want to hurt you," Randy said. "Let's do that again."

The second time was a little harder, but Mike finally pushed Randy's arm over again. Mike had a warm feeling inside. He felt scared, too. What if Randy was mad at him for winning?

"My arms are really strong from pushing my wheelchair around," Mike told Randy.

"No kidding," said Randy.

"It looks like the arm-wrestling champion of this class is Mike Stevens," Mrs. Kocher announced. "Tomorrow we'll have a checkers contest."

At the end of the day Randy walked over to Mike and said, "I suppose you're good at checkers, too?"

"I'm okay," said Mike. "At my old school we played checkers every day."

"Well, you may have won the arm-wrestling contest, but I play checkers with my sister. I always win." Randy went to meet his friends.

The next day in the cafeteria Susan sat down beside Mike. "Want a push back to the room?" she asked.

"Thanks, but I can push myself," answered Mike. "I wouldn't mind some company, though."

"Are you good enough to win at checkers, too?" Susan asked.

"I'm sure going to try," said Mike.

The checkers contest started right after lunch. Mike thought about every move he made. Finally it was just Mike and Randy. Then it was over, and Mrs. Kocher announced the winner. "Mike Stevens is our checkers champion. You gave him a good battle though, Randy." She smiled at both of them. Randy was smiling, too.

"What else can you do?" Randy asked Mike.

1. Why didn't Mike like his new school?

2. How did Mrs. Kocher help Mike?

3. How does the way Mike feels about himself change?

4. What kind of person do you think Mike is?

5. When did you know that Mike would win the arm-wrestling match?

6. It is important to be accepted as part of a group. How does Mike gain acceptance at his new school?

**Think
and
Write**

Prewrite

Although Mike was physically challenged and had to use a wheelchair, there were things that he could do well. Mike felt left out until he and his class realized he could do many of the same things they did, and even win at some things. Use the following chart to show how it feels to be part of the group and to be left out of a group.

FEELINGS	
Part of a Group	**Left Out of a Group**
_____	_____
_____	_____
_____	_____
_____	_____
_____	_____

Draft

Write about someone you think might feel different or left out. Don't use the person's real name. Why do you think that person feels that way? What are some of that person's strengths and some things that person is good at? What could be done to make him or her feel better?

Revise

One way to revise is to look over what you've written to see if you've really done all you were supposed to do. Add any details and information necessary to your story to make it complete.

278

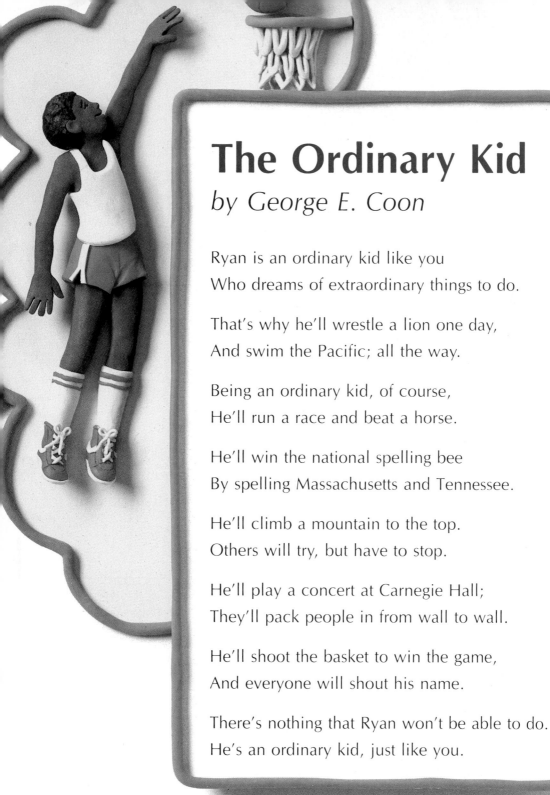

The Ordinary Kid
by George E. Coon

Ryan is an ordinary kid like you
Who dreams of extraordinary things to do.

That's why he'll wrestle a lion one day,
And swim the Pacific; all the way.

Being an ordinary kid, of course,
He'll run a race and beat a horse.

He'll win the national spelling bee
By spelling Massachusetts and Tennessee.

He'll climb a mountain to the top.
Others will try, but have to stop.

He'll play a concert at Carnegie Hall;
They'll pack people in from wall to wall.

He'll shoot the basket to win the game,
And everyone will shout his name.

There's nothing that Ryan won't be able to do.
He's an ordinary kid, just like you.

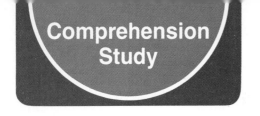

Cause and Effect

In some stories, authors tell how one thing causes another thing to happen. The **cause** tells *why* something happened and the **effect** tells *what* happened. Read the sentence below.

Since Mike can't use his legs, he will always need a wheelchair.

What is the result of Mike's not being able to use his legs? Mike will always need a wheelchair. Ask yourself *what* to find the effect, or result. Ask yourself *why* to find the cause, or reason.

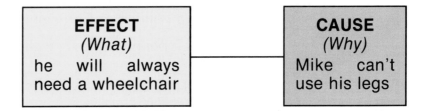

EFFECT *(What)* he will always need a wheelchair	**CAUSE** *(Why)* Mike can't use his legs

Sometimes several causes lead to one effect. Read the paragraph on the next page. Decide what the effect is. Then find three causes that led to the effect.

The population of California grew rapidly in the 1850's. Some people went to find gold. Some people moved from other places because of California's rich farmland. Still others went to find jobs.

What did you find out from the paragraph? You learned that the population of California grew rapidly in the 1850's. This is the effect, or what happened. What three things caused the population to grow at that time? People moved to California looking for gold. Other people moved there to farm. Some moved to California to find jobs. These are the causes or reasons why the population grew.

The boxes below show one way that will help you understand this cause-effect relationship.

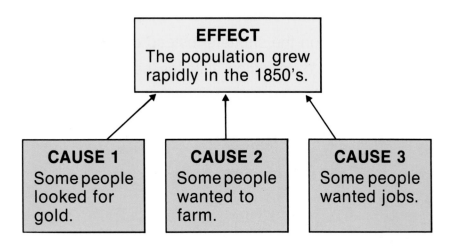

Remember that authors often use cause and effect to connect ideas. Look for cause-effect relationships to help you understand what you have read.

How does the truth cause changes in Tracy? How does the author help you see these changes?

The Girl Who Knew It All

by Patricia Reilly Giff

At the beginning of the summer, Tracy brought home a note from school that said she must read every day. Somehow Tracy never found the time to do this.

When Tracy saw that the shutters on an empty house down the street had been poorly painted, she tried to fix them. She misread the label on the can, and put red paint on the shutters instead of turpentine. Tracy didn't know that the new principal, Mrs. Bemus, was moving into the house.

As this story begins, Mrs. Bemus and Tracy are friends. Mrs. Bemus is taking Tracy and her sick dog to the vet.

The trip to the vet seemed to take forever. Finally Mrs. Bemus stopped in front of Dr. Wayne's office.

Tracy carried her quivering dog, Rebel, into the office.

Mrs. Wayne was in the reception room and said, "Take him right back into the doctor's office."

Dr. Wayne looked over his glasses at Tracy as she laid Rebel on the table. "I see you're still not watching what this dog eats," he said as he shook his head.

Dr. Wayne was touching Rebel carefully and looking in his eyes and ears and listening to his heart.

Finally he looked up and asked, "What have you fed this dog lately?"

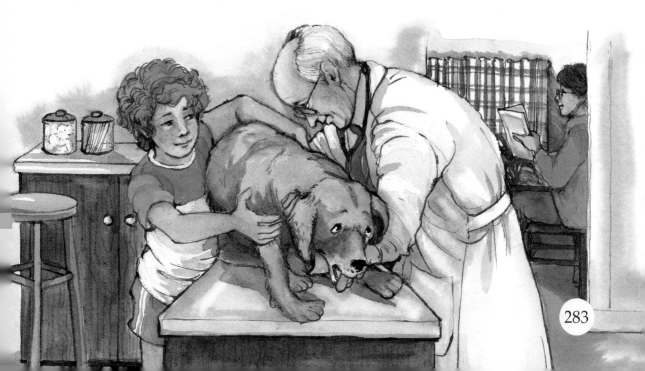

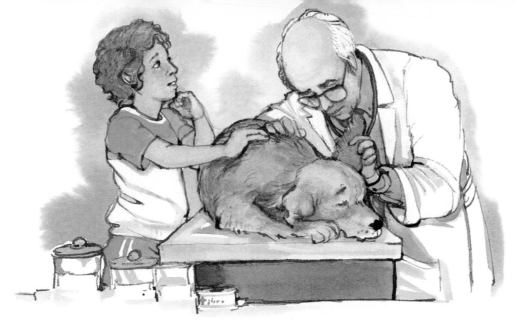

"Let's see." Tracy tried to remember. "We had cereal this morning. For supper last night my mother gave him dog food." For a minute she almost decided not to tell what she and Rebel had eaten for a snack last night, but then she sighed and blurted out the rest of the list. "Two pieces of pizza, one each, a bowl of popcorn, half a . . ."

"Enough," Dr. Wayne said. "An upset stomach. It's a wonder you don't have one, too. I'm going to give Rebel some medicine now to make his stomach feel better. Take the rest home and give it to him three times a day."

Tracy placed her hands under Rebel's quivering body and took the medicine from Dr. Wayne as she backed out of the room.

Mrs. Bemus was waiting in the reception room. "Is it anything serious?" she asked.

"He has an upset stomach," Tracy answered.

On the way home Mrs. Bemus asked, "What are
your friends doing on such a beautiful day?"

Tracy had almost forgotten. "Everyone is trying
to get money for the fair. They're putting on a
play," she said. Tracy tried to think of something
else to talk about. Finally she cleared her throat
and said, "Thank you for taking me to Dr. Wayne. I
was really worried about Rebel."

"Glad to do it, Tracy, since you've been such a
help to me."

She glanced at Mrs. Bemus to see if she was
serious. "I've been a help?"

"I found fish for my cat on the back porch three
times this week," Mrs. Bemus replied.

"I owed you," Tracy said without thinking.

For several seconds they did not speak. By now Mrs. Bemus was driving up High Flats Road. "I'm the one who painted your house," Tracy blurted out. "My reading's a mess, too."

Mrs. Bemus stopped the car in front of Tracy's house. She looked at Tracy seriously. "Why don't you put Rebel inside, and then come down to my house and we'll talk about it," she said.

Tracy lifted Rebel out of the car and closed the door with her hip. Inside, she laid Rebel gently on the living room rug. "You'll be all right," she said. "I have to see Mrs. Bemus, but I'll be back soon."

Before Tracy could even ring the bell, the screen door swung open. "Come on into the kitchen," Mrs. Bemus said. "Let's talk."

In the kitchen Tracy began, "I didn't mean . . . I couldn't read the label . . . I mean, I just wanted to fix the house up. Smooth it out with turpentine. I thought it was turpentine, but the paint can said *Turkey Red.*" Tracy glanced at Mrs. Bemus. Mrs. Bemus seemed to be staring at the floor.

Tracy began again. "All because I can't read. If I didn't have to read, everything would be perfect," she sighed. "Casey isn't going to be my friend any-more, and Leroy thinks I'm dumb. I'm not even going to be in the play, and it was all my idea . . ." her voice trailed off.

"All this happened because you're having trouble with reading?" Mrs. Bemus asked.

Tracy nodded, "It makes me get into all kinds of messes."

"Is that why you and Casey aren't friends anymore?"

"Well," she said, "Casey did say she'd help me with the reading."

"When is she going to start?"

Tracy lowered her head, "I told her I didn't want her help."

"All this because you're having trouble with reading," Mrs. Bemus said again.

"I . . ." Tracy said and stopped. Somehow that seemed backward. She was blaming all her problems on reading, but the truth was she was too lazy to practice her reading. She tried to make up for it by acting as if she knew everything in the whole round world.

Tracy took a deep breath and said, "I'm really sorry about your house. I was going to earn about a hundred dollars with the play and give you a whole bunch of money to get the house painted again."

Mrs. Bemus said, "You know, Tracy, I'm getting used to the house. No one else around here has red cabbages painted on the shutters."

"Cabbages! They were supposed to be roses," Tracy said.

Mrs. Bemus said, "Yes. I can see that now. I think I'll keep them. I didn't have the garage painted with the house. If you and some of those friends of yours want to make some money for the fair, I'd like to have you do it for me."

"Do you mean it? You could just pay the rest of the kids. It will make up for the first mess."

"That seems fair," Mrs. Bemus said. "Let me know when you're ready to begin."

After lunch, Tracy walked to Leroy's house.

"Want to help paint Mrs. Bemus's garage for money?"

Leroy said, "I suppose you'll be the boss."

"I don't have to be the boss," Tracy answered.

"All right," Leroy said. "Sure, I'll do it."

"How about getting Richard?" Tracy said. "We need all the hands we can get. Then meet me at Mrs. Bemus's garage and wait for me. I have to go see Casey."

She walked to Casey's house. "Casey!" she shouted.

Casey popped her head out of a window.

"Casey," she said again. "How would you like me to teach you how to paint a garage?"

Casey smiled back. "How would you like me to teach you how to read?"

"I'd like you to help me. I really would," Tracy replied.

Casey came down the steps. Tracy grabbed her hand, and together they ran toward the principal's house.

1. How does the truth cause changes in Tracy?

2. Why did Tracy's friends accept her again?

3. How did Mrs. Bemus help solve Tracy's problem?

4. How did you feel when Tracy was explaining her problems to Mrs. Bemus?

5. When did you know that Tracy would tell Mrs. Bemus the truth?

6. What truth did Tracy finally face?

**Think
and
Write**

Prewrite

Think about what kind of girl Tracy was. With a classmate, make a list of words to describe Tracy. Then copy the following idea burst onto a sheet of paper. On the lines connecting Tracy with the other characters, write two words from your list that each character might use to describe Tracy.

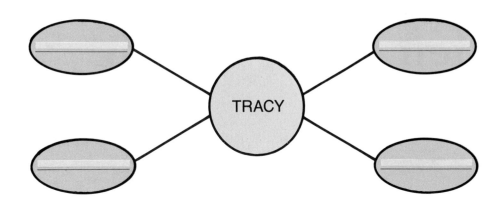

Draft

Pretend you are either Casey, Mrs. Bemus, Dr. Wayne, or Leroy. Thinking as the person you selected, write a description of Tracy. What kind of person is Tracy? How would you describe her? Use your completed idea burst for help in your writing.

Revise

Look over your writing carefully. Be sure you have described Tracy as that person would have described her. Add any detail that might make your description more complete.

How does a horseback ride teach Ellen a lesson?
What is the lesson that she learns?

John Newbery Honor Book Award

Ellen Rides Again
by Beverly Cleary

Ellen Tebbits and Austine Allen were best friends. They liked doing many things together.

Austine read many books about horses and wanted to ride one. Ellen didn't know much about horses but had ridden several times. As the story begins, the girls are at the library talking about horses.

At the library Austine had been lucky enough to find two horse books. "I wish I could ride a horse sometime," she said.

"Haven't you ever ridden a horse?" asked Ellen.

"No. Have you?" Austine sounded impressed.

"Oh, yes," said Ellen casually. "Several times."

It was true. She had ridden several times. If she had ridden twice, she would have said a couple of times. Three was several times, so she had told the truth.

"Where? What was it like? Tell me about it," begged Austine.

"Oh, different places." That was also true. She had ridden at the beach. Her father had rented a horse for an hour and had let Ellen ride behind him with her arms around his waist. The horse's back had been slippery, and she had bounced harder than was comfortable, but she had been able to hang on.

She had ridden at Uncle Fred's farm. Uncle Fred had lifted her up onto the back of his old plow horse, Lady, and led her twice around the barnyard. Lady didn't bounce her at all.

Then there was that other time when her father had paid a dime so she could ride a pony around in a circle inside a fence. It hadn't been very exciting. The pony seemed tired, but Ellen had pretended it was galloping madly. Yes, it all added up to several times.

"Why haven't you told me you could ride?" Austine demanded. "What kind of saddle do you use?" Austine knew all about different kinds of saddles because she read so many horse books.

"Oh, any kind," said Ellen, who did not know one saddle from another. "Once I rode bareback." That was true, because Lady had no saddle. Ellen was beginning to feel a little uncomfortable. She had not meant to mislead Austine. She really did not know how it all started.

The next day at school Austine did not forget what Ellen had said about being able to ride a horse. She told Linda and Amelia about it. They told Barbara and George. Barbara and George told other boys and girls. Each time the story was told, it grew.

After school, when the girls came to Austine's house, they found Mrs. Allen on her knees beside a box of plants. "Hello there," she said. "Since tomorrow is Memorial Day and there isn't any school, how would you like to go on a picnic? Ellen, I have already asked your mother and she says you may go."

"Thank you. I'd love to go." Maybe a picnic would make Austine forget about horses. Ellen was worried that Austine might say something about horseback riding to Ellen's mother, and her mother would know how Ellen had exaggerated.

The next morning at ten o'clock Ellen ran down Tillamook Street and around the corner to Austine's house. Mr. Allen was backing out the car. Mrs. Allen sat in the front seat. Ellen was glad she and Austine could each sit by a window in the back. That made it easier to look for horses and to play word games.

They had only driven a few miles when Austine saw the horses. "Look, Daddy! Horses for rent! Please stop," she begged.

Mr. Allen drew over to the side of the road near some horses in a corral. Austine jumped out of the car and ran to the horses, while the others followed.

"Daddy, please let us go horseback riding!" Ellen wished Austine would keep still.

"All right, girls. Which horses do you want to ride?" asked Mr. Allen.

Ellen thought she had better act brave even if she didn't feel that way. "I think I'd like the brown one over in the corner of the pen." She thought the brown horse looked gentle.

"I'll take the pinto," said Austine.

"Oh dear," thought Ellen. "I've said the wrong thing. I wish I'd read some horse books."

When the horses were ready, the man who worked at the stables held out his hand, palm up, for Ellen to step into. She put her foot into his hand, and he boosted her onto the horse. The ground seemed a long way below her. Ellen had forgotten how wide a horse was. The man shortened her stirrups and then helped Austine onto the pinto. Ellen patted her horse on the neck. She was anxious to have him like her.

"Look," cried Austine. "I'm really on a horse!"

Ellen knew she was expected to take the lead. "Giddap," she said. The horse did not move.

The man gave each horse a light slap on the rump. They walked out of the corral and down the dirt road as if they were used to going that way. Austine's mother and father followed on foot.

Ellen carefully held one rein in each hand. As she looked at the ground so far below, she hoped the horse wouldn't decide to run.

"I'm going to call my horse Old Paint like in the song," said Austine, who knew about cowboy songs. "Why don't you call yours Brownie?"

"Yes," said Ellen. She didn't feel like talking.

When Austine's horse moved in front, Ellen took hold of the saddle horn. It wasn't so much that she was scared, she told herself. She just didn't want to take any chances.

Maybe this wasn't going to be so bad after all. The horses seemed to know the way, and Ellen found the rocking back and forth to be pleasant. She was even able to look around at the trees and enjoy the woodsy smell.

Then when they had gone around a curve, Brownie wanted to go back to the corral. He turned around and started walking back.

"Hey," said Ellen anxiously. She pulled on the right rein, but Brownie kept on going. "Stop!" she ordered, more loudly this time.

"Why are you going that way?" asked Austine, turning in her saddle.

"Because the horse wants to," said Ellen crossly.

"Well, turn him around."

"I can't," said Ellen. "He won't steer."

Austine turned Old Paint and drew up beside Ellen.

"Don't you know you're supposed to hold both reins in one hand?"

Ellen didn't know. "I just held them this way to try to turn him," she said. Ellen took the reins in her left hand.

Austine leaned over and took hold of Brownie's bridle with one hand. "Come on, Old Paint," she said. Brownie followed.

"Thanks," said Ellen. "My, you're brave."

"Oh, that's nothing," said Austine. "You don't steer a horse," she added, "you guide him."

"Oh . . . I forgot." What would Austine think when she found out how Ellen had misled her?

The horses plodded down the road. Through the trees the girls could see the highway and hear cars passing. Austine's mother and father came around the corner, and Ellen began to feel brave again.

"Let's gallop," suggested Austine.

Ellen's legs were beginning to ache. "How do you make them gallop?"

"Dig your heels in," said Austine.

"I wouldn't want to hurt the horse," said Ellen.

"You won't hurt him, silly. Cowboys wear spurs, don't they?"

Ellen timidly kicked Brownie with her heels. Brownie walked slowly on.

Austine dug in her heels. Old Paint began to trot. At first Austine bounced, but soon she rode smoothly. Then her horse began to gallop.

When Old Paint galloped, Brownie began to trot. Ellen began to bounce. She hung onto the saddle horn as hard as she could. Still she bounced. Slap-slap-slap. Her bare legs began to hurt from rubbing against the leather of the saddle flap. Slap-slap-slap. "Goodness, I sound awful," she thought. "I hope Austine doesn't hear me slapping this way."

"Whoa, Old Paint!" cried Austine. Old Paint stopped.

"I did it, Ellen!" she called. "I really, truly galloped. I hung on with my knees and galloped just like in the movies."

"Wh-wh-oa-oa!" Ellen cried. Brownie trotted on. Slap-slap-slap.

Austine began to laugh. "I can see trees between you and the saddle every time you go up. Oh, Ellen, you look so funny!"

Slap-slap-slap. Ellen didn't think she could stand much more bouncing.

"Ellen Tebbits! I don't think you know a thing about horseback riding."

"Wh-wh-oa-oa!" When Brownie reached Old Paint, he stopped. After Ellen got her breath, she cried, "I do, too. It's just that the other horses I rode were tamer."

The horses walked on until the road curved down to the edge of a stream.

"Oh, look. There's a bridge," exclaimed Ellen.

"I guess the highway crosses to the other side of the stream," said Austine. "I wonder if the poor horses would like to drink."

There was no doubt about Brownie's wanting a drink. He left the road and picked his way down the rocky bank to the water. Brownie did not stop at the edge of the stream. He walked out into it.

"Whoa!" yelled Ellen, above the rush of the water. "Austine, help!"

Brownie walked on.

"Austine! What'll I do? He's going swimming!"

"Here, Brownie! Here, Brownie!" called Austine from the bank. Her voice sounded faint across the water.

When Brownie had found his way around the boulders to the middle of the stream, he stopped.

"Look, he's in over his knees!" Ellen looked down at the water. "Giddap, Brownie!"

"Slap him on the rump with the ends of the reins," directed Austine from the bank.

Ellen slapped. Brownie turned his head and looked at her. By this time some hikers had stopped on the

bridge. Looking down at Ellen, they laughed and pointed. Ellen wished they would go away.

Brownie lowered his head to drink. Because Ellen had the reins wound around her hand, she could not let go. As she was pulled forward, the saddle horn poked her in the stomach.

"Oof," she said. Hanging over the horse's neck, she clung to his mane with one hand.

Brownie looked at her with water dripping from his chin. Ellen thought it was his chin. Maybe on a horse it was called something else.

A couple of cars stopped on the bridge, and the people looked down at Ellen and laughed. "Do something, Austine," Ellen called. "Our half hour must be nearly up."

"Maybe I could ride back and get the man who owns the horses," Austine yelled back.

"No, Austine. Don't leave me here alone," begged Ellen. "Maybe I could get off. I don't think the water would come up to my shoulders."

"The current's too strong," called Austine. "Anyway, we're supposed to bring the horses back. You can't go off and leave Brownie."

Austine was right. Ellen knew that she couldn't leave Brownie. She might lose him, and the man would probably make her pay for him. She had never heard of anyone losing a horse, so she wasn't sure. "I can't stay here forever," she called.

"Mother and Daddy should catch up with us in a minute," Austine called. "They'll know what to do."

That was just what was worrying Ellen. She didn't want the Allens to see her like this. What would they think after Austine had told them she had ridden before?

One of the hikers climbed down the bank to the edge of the water. "Need some help?" he called.

"Oh yes, please," answered Ellen thankfully.

Jumping from boulder to boulder, the man came near her, but he could not get close enough to reach Brownie's bridle. "Throw me the reins," he called.

Ellen threw them as hard as she could. The man grabbed them as the current carried them toward him.

"Come on, old fellow," he said, pulling at the reins. Slowly Brownie began to find his way around the boulders toward the bank.

"Oh, thank you," said Ellen.

"The trouble is, you let the horse know you were afraid of him," said the man. "Let the old nag know you're boss and you won't have any trouble."

"Thank you, I'll try," said Ellen, taking a firm hold on the reins. "Good-bye."

Just then Austine's mother and father came around the corner in the road. "It's time to turn back now," said Mrs. Allen.

"All right, Mother," said Austine. The girls headed their horses toward the corral. Ellen felt bad and she didn't know what to say to Austine. What would Austine think of her after she knew Ellen had exaggerated? What would Austine tell her parents? What would she tell the kids at school?

Finally, Ellen said in a low voice, "I guess I didn't

know quite as much about horseback riding as I thought I did."

"Your horse was just hard to handle, that's all," said Austine.

"Austine?" said Ellen timidly.

"What?"

"You won't tell anybody, will you?"

Austine smiled at her. "Of course I won't tell. We're best friends, aren't we? It'll be our secret. Giddap, Old Paint."

"Thank you," said Ellen. "You're a wonderful friend. You know what? I'm going to look for horse books the next time we go the library."

If you want to find out more about Ellen and Austine, read Ellen Tebbits *by Beverly Cleary.*

1. What lesson does Ellen learn in this story?

2. What trouble does Ellen have when she and Austine go horseback riding?

3. How does Ellen get Brownie out of the stream?

4. Do you think Austine is a good best friend? Why?

5. How did you know that Austine wouldn't have any trouble with horseback riding?

6. Do you think Ellen felt bad about exaggerating? Explain your answer.

Thinking About "Milestones"

In this unit, you read about people who met milestones that changed their lives. Some of the stories are about times that were the foundation of our country's history. Sally and her family set out to be pioneers in Maine. The story of Old Sturbridge Village tells how one man's idea continues to provide visitors with a view of what life was like in early America.

Other stories tell about personal milestones that the major characters met in their lives. Mike Stevens proved himself at his new school. Ellen had to admit that she exaggerated. She also learned what it means to have a good friend.

In "Milestones," the characters faced challenges that caused them to show courage and strength. They all reached important milestones in their lives. As you read other stories, decide what milestones the characters reach and what these milestones mean to them.

1. Sally and Mike Stevens are faced with similar milestones. What is the challenge that each must face? How does each character react to the challenge?

2. How are Tracy's situation and Maggie's situation the same? How are their situations different?

3. Both Tracy and Ellen act in ways that are not completely honest. Explain what each character learns about herself.

4. What did Francisco Gabilondo Soler do in his lifetime that is similar to what Albert Wells did when he created Old Sturbridge Village?

5. Tracy and Mike Stevens were faced with different milestones. Explain the differences in their situations.

Glossary

The glossary is a special dictionary for this book. The glossary tells you how to spell a word, how to pronounce it, and what the word means. Often the word is used in a sentence. Different forms of the word may be given. If one of the different forms is used in the book, then that form is used in the sentence.

A blue box ■ at the end of the entry tells you that an illustration is given for that word.

The following abbreviations are used throughout the glossary; *n.,* noun; *v.,* verb; *adj.,* adjective; *adv.,* adverb; *interj.,* interjection; *prep.,* preposition; *conj.,* conjunction; *pl.,* plural; *sing.,* singular; *syn.,* synonym; *syns.,* synonyms.

An accent mark (') is used to show which syllable receives the most stress. For example, in the word *granite* [gran' it], the first syllable receives more stress. Sometimes in words of two or more syllables, there is also a lighter mark to show that a syllable receives a lighter stress. For example, in the word *helicopter* [hel'ə·kop'tər], the first syllable has the most stress, and the third syllable has lighter stress.

The symbols used to show how each word is pronounced are explained in the "Pronunciation Key" on the next page.

Pronunciation Key*

a	add, map	m	move, seem	u	up, done
ā	ace, rate	n	nice, tin	û(r)	burn, term
â(r)	care, air	ng	ring, song	yo͞o	fuse, few
ä	palm, father	o	odd, hot	v	vain, eve
b	bat, rub	ō	open, so	w	win, away
ch	check, catch	ô	order, jaw	y	yet, yearn
d	dog, rod	oi	oil, boy	z	zest, muse
e	end, pet	ou	pout, now	zh	vision, pleasure
ē	equal, tree	o͝o	took, full	ə	the schwa,
f	fit, half	o͞o	pool, food		an unstressed
g	go, log	p	pit, stop		vowel representing
h	hope, hate	r	run, poor		the sound spelled
i	it, give	s	see, pass	a	in *above*
ī	ice, write	sh	sure, rush	e	in *sicken*
j	joy, ledge	t	talk, sit	i	in *possible*
k	cool, take	th	thin, both	o	in *melon*
l	look, rule	t̶h̶	this, bathe	u	in *circus*

*Adapted entries, the Pronunciation Key, and the Short Key that appear on the following pages are reprinted from *HBJ School Dictionary*, copyright © 1985 by Harcourt Brace Jovanovich, Inc. Reprinted by permission of Harcourt Brace Jovanovich, Inc.

A

adapt [ə·dapt′] *v.* **adapted** To change and make suitable for a new use: We *adapted* the crate for a rabbit cage.

agent [ā′jənt] *n., pl.* **agents** A person who can act for someone else: The ticket *agent* told me the plane was late. *syn.* representative

aisle [īl] *n., pl.* **aisles** A path between rows of seats: No one should stand in the *aisles;* everyone should sit. *syn.* passageway ■

amazing [ə·mā′zing] *adj.* Causing a feeling of surprise or bewilderment: Some of the new things the inventor made were really *amazing.* *syns.* surprising, astonishing

announce [ə·nouns′] *v.* **announced, announcing** To say in public for all to hear: Mr. Rice *announced* that Ms. Kent is our new teacher. *syns.* broadcast, declare

anxious [angk′shəs] *adj.* **anxiously** *adv.* Worried: We *anxiously* waited for the test reports. *syns.* worried, troubled

area [âr′ē·ə] *n., pl.* **areas** A space used for a certain purpose: We will meet in the open *area* near the school.

arithmetic [ə·rith′mə·tik] *n.* The study of numbers and how to use them to add, subtract, multiply, and divide: Charlie is very good at *arithmetic,* so we put him in charge of the money.

arrange [ə·rānj′] *v.* **arranged, arranging** To put into a certain order: We *arranged* the books on the shelf.

arrive [ə·rīv′] *v.* **arrived, arriving** To get to a place: Sasha *arrived* home late. *syn.* reach

astronomer [ə·stron′ə·mər] *n., pl.* **astronomers** A person who studies the stars and planets: *Astronomers* usually work at night. *syn.* stargazer

autumn [ô′təm] *n.* The fall of the year: We go back to school in the *autumn. syn.* fall

---

B

---

bale [bāl] *n., pl.* **bales** A large bundle of cotton, hay, or other material: We put the *bales* of hay in the barn. *syn.* bundle

banjo [ban′jō] *n., pl.* **banjos** or **banjoes** A musical instrument with strings: Tunes played on a *banjo* are very lively. ■

barnacle [bär′nə·kəl] *n., pl.* **barnacles** A sea creature that sticks itself to boats, rocks, and other creatures: I picked a *barnacle* off the bottom of the boat.

boulder [bōl′dər] *n., pl.* **boulders** A large rock: Our yard goes up to those *boulders* by the road. *syn.* rock

bridle [brīd′(ə)l] *n., pl.* **bridles** The part of a horse's harness that fits around the head: Shari put the *bridle* on the horse. ■

burdock [bûr′dok] *n.* A burr plant: I got burrs all over my sweater when I fell against the *burdock.* ■

a	add	o	odd	oi	oil
ā	ace	ō	open	ou	pout
â	care	ô	order	ng	ring
ä	palm	ŏŏ	took	th	thin
e	end	ōō	pool	th	this
ē	equal	u	up	zh	vision
i	it	û	burn		
ī	ice	yōō	fuse		

ə = { a in *above* e in *sicken* i in *possible*
o in *melon* u in *circus* }

bury [ber′ē] *v.* **buried, burying** To put into the ground: Dogs sometimes *bury* their bones. *syns.* cover, hide

C

caboose [kə·bōōs′] *n., pl.* **cabooses** A car at the end of a train used by the crew: The *caboose* is often painted red.

cafeteria [kaf′ə·tir′ē·ə] *n., pl.* **cafeterias** A kind of restaurant where people serve themselves by choosing from food on display: Lets have lunch in the *cafeteria. syns.* lunchroom, restaurant

carrier [kar′ē·ər] *n., pl.* **carriers** A large ship that carries airplanes which both land and take off from it: The sailor stood on the deck of the aircraft *carrier.*

carve [kärv] *v.* **carved, carving** To cut designs or letters on something: Flowers were *carved* into the wood. *syn.* cut

casual [kazh′ōō·əl] *adj.* **casually** *adv.* Without plan: He painted the picture *casually. syn.* unexpected

catalogue [kat′ə·lôg] *n., pl.* **catalogues** A book showing things for sale: Meg often ordered clothes from *catalogues.*

catwalk [kat′wôk′] *n., pl.* **catwalks** A high, narrow walk, such as that alongside a bridge: We walked carefully along the *catwalk. syn.* walkway ■

chamber [chām′bər] *n., pl.* **chambers** A room: Your sleeping *chambers* are right down the hall. *syns.* room, hall

cluster [klus′tər] *n., pl.* **clusters** A group of similar things: There is a *cluster* of daisies by the tree. *syn.* group

concern [kən·sûrn′] *v.* **concerned, concerning** To worry: He is *concerned* about the test.

conductor [kən·duk′tər] *n., pl.* **conductors** The person who is in charge of a bus or train: The *conductor* took our tickets.

conservatory [kən·sûr′və·tôr′ē] *n., pl.* **conservatories** A greenhouse where plants are grown: I grew this rose in the *conservatory*. *syn.* greenhouse

control panel [kən·trōl′ pan′əl] *n., pl.* **control panels** A board from which a system or vehicle is run: Sue sat at the *control panel* and turned on the stage lights. ■

corral [kə·ral′] *n., pl.* **corrals** A fenced-in area for cows, horse, or sheep: Please open the gate to the *corral* and let the horses out. *syn.* pen

crater [krā′tər] *n., pl.* **craters** A hollow area around a volcano: The *craters* were very deep.

create [krē·āt′] *v.* **created, creating 1** To make: the artist *created* the painting. *syns.* make, originate **2** To cause: Linn's lying *created* a problem. *syn.* cause

creature [krē′chər] *n., pl.* **creatures** A living thing: I could not see what the *creature* was, but I think it was a dog. *syn.* being

culture [kul′chər] *n., pl.* **cultures** The history, customs, and ideas of a group of people: Many wonderful songs have come to us from the Irish *culture*.

a	add	o	odd	oi	oil
ā	ace	ō	open	ou	pout
â	care	ô	order	ng	ring
ä	palm	o͝o	took	th	thin
e	end	o͞o	pool	th	this
ē	equal	u	up	zh	vision
i	it	û	burn		
ī	ice	yo͞o	fuse		

ə = { a in *above* e in *sicken* i in *possible*
      o in *melon* u in *circus* }

current [kûr′ənt] *n., pl.* **currents** A part of water or air that moves in a certain direction: The air *currents* carried the balloon far away. *syn.* stream

curve [kûrv] *n., pl.* **curves** A smooth bend: There is a *curve* in the road by our house. *syn.* bend

custom [kus′təm] *n., pl.* **customs** An accepted practice followed by a group of people: Parades and fireworks are two July Fourth *customs.* *syns.* habit, practice

cylinder [sil′in·dər] *n., pl.* **cylinders** A part of a machine: The *cylinders* help the machine to run. ■

D

declare [di·klâr′] *v.* **declared, declaring** To say with force;

announce: Mr. Wong *declared* that he had never seen a better play. *syns.* state, say

determine [di·tûr′min] *v.* To find out: We used a map to *determine* how far we were from the city.

devotion [di·vō′shən] *n.* Loyalty; dedication: Her *devotion* to music has lasted all her life.

disappear [dis′ə·pir′] *v.* **disappeared, disappearing** To go out of sight, sometimes suddenly: The rabbit *disappeared* when the magician said the magic words. *syn.* vanish

doubt [dout] *n., pl.* **doubts** The lack of being sure about something: Without a *doubt,* this is the best loaf of bread. *syn.* uncertainty

E

embroider [im·broi′dər] *v.* **embroidered, embroidering** To decorate with fancy sewing: My grandmother *embroidered* beautiful designs. *syn.* sew

engineer [en'jə·nir'] *n., pl.* **engineers** A person who runs a train: The *engineer* slowed down as he came around the bend.

entrance [en'trəns] *n., pl.* **entrances** A door or gate used for going into a place: Wait for me by the *entrance*. *syns.* doorway, entry

event [i·vent'] *n., pl.* **events** A happening: The Fourth of July parade is a special *event* in our town. *syn.* happening

exaggerate [ig·zaj'ə·rāt'] *v.* **exaggerated, exaggerating** To make something seem more than it is: Biff *exaggerated* when he said his dog was huge; it's really quite small. *syns.* magnify, overstate

experience [ik·spir'ē·əns] *v.* **experienced, experiencing** To feel or live through: I would like to *experience* life on another planet.

experiment [ik·sper'ə·mənt] *n., pl.* **experiments** A test done in order to learn or prove something: Stacy's *experiments* with insects taught her what those creatures eat. *syns.* test, tryout

explanation [ek'splə·nā'shən] *n., pl.* **explanations** A reason that makes something understood: That's the *explanation* of the missing money. *syn.* reason

explode [ik·splōd'] *v.* **exploded, exploding** To burst: The car could *explode* if it catches on fire. *syn.* blow up

explosive [ik·splō'siv] *n., pl.* **explosives** A material that explodes, or blows up: The workers set off the *explosives* to clear the road.

F

faint [fānt] *adj.* Weak: The noise was so *faint* I could hardly hear it. *syn.* weak

a	add	o	odd	oi	oil
ā	ace	ō	open	ou	pout
â	care	ô	order	ng	ring
ä	palm	ŏŏ	took	th	thin
e	end	ōō	pool	th	this
ē	equal	u	up	zh	vision
i	it	û	burn		
ī	ice	yōō	fuse		

ə = { a in *above*   e in *sicken*   i in *possible*
      o in *melon*   u in *circus* }

fashion [fash'ən] *n.* The style of clothing at a certain time: Sneakers are a popular *fashion* lately.

fetch [fech] *v.* **fetched, fetching** To get someone or something and bring it back: Will you please *fetch* me the blanket? *syn.* bring

figurehead [fig'yər·hed] *n., pl.* **figureheads** A carving of a person or animal on the front of a sailing ship: Old ships often have *figureheads.* *syn.* statue ■

glow [glō] *v.* To shine because of great heat: Many comets *glow.*

gorgeous [gôr'jəs] *adj.* Very beautiful: The sunset last night was *gorgeous.* *syns.* beautiful, stunning

grant [grant] *v.* **granted, granting** To give: My mother always *grants* me one special wish on my birthday. *syns.* give, allow

gull [gul] *n., pl.* **gulls** A sea bird: The *gull* picked up a fish in its bill. ■

gurgle [gûr'gəl] *v.* **gurgled, gurgling** To make a low, bubbling sound: The water was *gurgling* in the sink.

G

glorious [glôr'ē·əs] *adj.* Very beautiful; splendid: It was a *glorious* month of June. *syn.* splendid

H

headache [hed'āk'] *n., pl.* **headaches** A pain in the head: I have a *headache* because I haven't eaten lunch.

healthy [hel′thē] *adj.* **healthiest** Having or showing good health: Bill is the *healthiest* person in his family.

heavenly [hev′ən·lē] *adj.* In space: The closest *heavenly* body to the earth is the moon.

heroine [her′ō·in] *n., pl.* **heroines** **1** A female who is known for her courage: Eleanor Roosevelt is an American *heroine*. **2** The main female character in a story: Charlotte is the *heroine* of *Charlotte's Web.*

heron [her′ən] *n., pl.* **herons** A wading bird with long legs: The *heron* walked along the beach. ■

history [his′tə·rē] *n.* The study of the past: Geraldo is studying the *history* of the town where he lives.

I

identify [ī·den′tə·fī′] *v.* To recognize a certain thing: Can you *identify* your street?

impress [im·pres′] *v.* **impressed, impressing** To have an effect on the feelings or thoughts of: I was *impressed* by the woman who spoke to us. *syns.* affect, influence

industry [in′dəs·trē] *n., pl.* **industries** A business: The town grew when new *industries* opened.

iron [ī′ərn] *n.* A strong metal: The fire did not get past the *iron* door.

a	add	o	odd	oi	oil
ā	ace	ō	open	ou	pout
â	care	ô	order	ng	ring
ä	palm	o͝o	took	th	thin
e	end	o͞o	pool	t̶h̶	this
ē	equal	u	up	zh	vision
i	it	û	burn		
ī	ice	yo͞o	fuse		

ə = { a in *above*   e in *sicken*   i in *possible*
       o in *melon*   u in *circus* }

island [ī′lənd] *n., pl.* **islands** A body of land surrounded by water: We can walk to those *islands* at low tide. ■

item [ī′təm] *n., pl.* **items** Any one thing in a group: She put out all the *items* she needed to make the meal.

ivory [ī′vər·ē] *n.* A hard, white material of which elephants' and walruses' tusks are made: We saw beautiful jewelry made from *ivory*.

J

jacket [jak′it] *n., pl.* **jackets** The outside covering, such as that on a book: The book's *jacket* showed a picture of the author.

jetty [jet′ē] *n., pl.* **jetties** A stone or wooden structure that sticks out into the water:

The *jetty* made our beach better for swimming. *syns.* dock, wharf ■

junk [jungk] *n., pl.* **junks** A large flat-bottomed Chinese boat: There were many *junks* in the water. *syn.* boat ■

K

kerchief [kûr′chif] *n., pl.* **kerchiefs** A piece of cloth usually worn over a person's head: Lara tied a *kerchief* over her hair to keep it dry. *syn.* bandanna

L

leather [leth′ər] *n.* Animal skin that has been cleaned and tanned for use in such things as clothing and shoes: My jacket is made of brown *leather.*

length [leng(k)th] *n.* The measure from end to end: He ran the *length* of the field.

level [lev′əl] **1** *v.* **leveled, leveling** To make a flat, even surface: There were hills, then the land *leveled* off to flat fields. *syns.* flatten, smooth **2** *n., pl.* **levels** Depth or height: The water reached a *level* of six inches. *syns.* depth, height

limb [lim] *n., pl.* **limbs** An arm, leg, or wing: The seal has a sore *limb.*

lobster-like [lob′stər·līk′] *adj.* Like a lobster: The animal had a *lobster-like* claw.

locomotive [lō′kə·mō′tiv] *n., pl.* **locomotives** An engine that pulls a train: His father drives a *locomotive. syn.* engine

lupine [loo′pin] *n., pl.* **lupines** A plant with long clusters of flowers: This *lupine* has blue flowers. ■

M

magnificent [mag·nif′ə·sənt] *adj.* Splendid, grand: Their new house is *magnificent. syns.* grand, majestic, splendid, superb

manage [man′ij] *v.* **managed, managing 1** To control: Mrs. Olivera *managed* the store. *syn.* control **2** To get done or get by: I *managed* to get home, even though it took three hours.

a	add	o	odd	oi	oil
ā	ace	ō	open	ou	pout
â	care	ô	order	ng	ring
ä	palm	ŏŏ	took	th	thin
e	end	ōō	pool	th	this
ē	equal	u	up	zh	vision
i	it	û	burn		
ī	ice	yōō	fuse		

ə = { a in *above* e in *sicken* i in *possible* { o in *melon* u in *circus*

mare [mâr] *n., pl.* **mares** A female horse: We hitched the *mare* to the wagon. *syn.* horse

masquerader [mas′kə·rād′ər] *n., pl.* **masqueraders** A person who pretends to be someone else by wearing a disguise or a costume: The *masqueraders* took off their masks.

mathematician [math′ə·mə·tish′ən] *n., pl.* **mathematicians** A person who studies mathematics: Mr. Kraus is a *mathematician* working on the space program.

mathematics [math′ə·mat′iks] *n.* The study of numbers and other symbols that stand for them: Mrs. Lane teaches *mathematics* at the high school. *syn.* arithmetic

measure [mezh′ər] *v.* **measured, measuring** To find out the size of something, using a system of counting units: I *measured* the girl to see how tall she was. *syn.* gauge

melody [mel′ə·dē] *n., pl.* **melodies** A series of musical notes; tune: The *melodies* of those two songs are similar. *syns.* tune, song

messenger [mes′ən·jər] *n., pl.* **messengers** A person sent to bring a message or to do an errand: The *messenger* brought a letter to Mrs. Bunting.

misread [mis·rēd′] *v.* **misread, misreading** To read incorrectly: Did she *misread* the instructions?

murmur [mûr′mər] *v.* **murmured, murmuring** To speak in a soft, unclear voice: "I'm afraid," the child was able to *murmur. syns.* whisper, mumble

mussel [mus′əl] *n., pl.* **mussels** A kind of shellfish that looks like a clam: The *mussel* was found in a tide pool. ∎

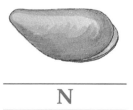

N

naturally [nach′ər·əl·ē] *adv.* Of course: "*Naturally,* I cooked your favorite food," said Uncle Ed. *syn.* certainly

navigator [nav′ə·gā′·tər] *n., pl.* **navigators** A person who plans the course of a plane or a ship: The *navigator* told us to sail into the wind.

No. The abbreviation for *number:* Is this the *No.* 78 bus?

O

observatory [əb·zûr′və·tôr′ē] *n., pl.* **observatories** A building from which the stars and other natural things, such as weather, are studied: The people at the *observatory* say that rain is on the way. *syn.* lookout ■

old-fashioned [old′fash′ənd] *adj.* Of an earlier time: My aunt loves *old-fashioned* cars. *syns.* outdated, obsolete

one-and-one-half [wun′ənd· wun·haf′] *n., adj.* A unit and a half of a unit: My dog is *one-and-one-half* feet tall.

P

parachute [par′ə·shoot′] *n., pl.* **parachutes** A device somewhat similar to an umbrella used to slow down the fall of an object: Their *parachutes* opened and they floated down slowly. ■

passage [pas′ij] *n.* The act of passing: The *passage* from winter to spring is beautiful.

a	add	o	odd	oi	oil
ā	ace	ō	open	ou	pout
â	care	ô	order	ng	ring
ä	palm	o͝o	took	th	thin
e	end	o͞o	pool	t͟h	this
ē	equal	u	up	zh	vision
i	it	û	burn		
ī	ice	yo͞o	fuse		

ə = { a in *above*   e in *sicken*   i in *possible*
     o in *melon*   u in *circus*

passenger [pas'ən·jər] *n., pl.* **passengers** A person who rides in a train, bus, boat, plane, or car: The *passengers* in the plane were given something to eat. *syns.* rider, traveler

pinto [pin'tō] *n., pl.* **pintos** A kind of spotted horse or pony: Luke will ride the *pinto.*

piston [pis'tən] *n., pl.* **pistons** A part of a machine that moves up and down in a tube: The machine came to a stop when the *pistons* broke. ■

platform [plat'fôrm'] *n., pl.* **platforms** A flat floor or surface higher than what is around it: We could see the ocean from the *platform. syn.* stage

pleasant [plez'ənt] *adj.* Enjoyable; agreeable: Yesterday it rained, but today it is *pleasant. syn.* agreeable

plod [plod] *v.* **plodded, plodding** To walk in a slow, heavy way: We *plodded* through the deep snow. *syn.* trudge

pluck [pluck] *v.* **plucking** To quickly pull and let go: Alison is *plucking* the strings on the guitar.

potion [pō'shən] *n., pl.* **potions** A liquid that is supposed to have medicinal or magic powers: The wizard liked to make magic *potions.*

presence [prez'əns] *n.* **1** The state of being present: Your *presence* at the party is important to me. **2** The area around someone: Don't talk in Mr. Donnelly's *presence.*

produce [prə·d(y)oos'] *v.* **producing** To bring into being: These trees are *producing* fruit.

Q

quiver [kwiv'ər] *v.* **quivered, quivering** To tremble or shake: When I saw her *quivering* lips, I knew Carly was nervous. *syns.* shake, quake

R

raven [rā'vən] *n., pl.* **ravens 1** *n.* A large, black, shiny bird: The *raven* sat on the wall. **2** *adj.* Shiny black: Terry had *raven* hair and brown eyes. ∎

razor [ra'zər] *n., pl.* **razors** A sharp blade made for cutting off hair: The man shaved his face with a *razor*.

reception [ri·sep'shən] *adj.* Greeting; meeting: The *reception* area is where guests sign in. *syn.* gathering

recover [ri·kuv'ər] *v.* **recovered, recovering** To get better from an illness: I have *recovered* from my cold.

rein [rān] *n., pl.* **reins** A long strap used by a rider to guide a horse: Each *rein* is attached to a bit in the horse's mouth. *syn.* leash

rely [ri·lī'] *v.* **relied, relying** To depend on: I can always *rely* on my friend for help. *syn.* depend

repay [ri·pā'] *v.* **repaid, repaying** To pay back: Marc *repaid* us by cutting the grass.

request [ri·kwest'] *n., pl.* **requests** Something asked for: The wizard said, "I will give you one *request.*"

responsible [ri·spon'sə·bəl] *adj.* Being the reason for or cause of something: The snowy weather was *responsible* for our missing so much school. *syns.* answerable, accountable, liable

rhythm [rith'əm] *n.* The beat: The drums played the *rhythm* of the song.

a	add	o	odd	oi	oil
ā	ace	ō	open	ou	pout
â	care	ô	order	ng	ring
ä	palm	ŏŏ	took	th	thin
e	end	ōō	pool	th	this
ē	equal	u	up	zh	vision
i	it	û	burn		
ī	ice	yōō	fuse		

ə = { a in *above*   e in *sicken*   i in *possible*
      o in *melon*   u in *circus* }

S

satisfy [sat′is·fī] *v.* **satisfied, satisfying** To supply what is wanted; to please: I was *satisfied* when I saw how well we had done. *syns.* please, gratify

scientist [sī′ən·tist] *n., pl.* **scientists** A person who is an expert in science: The *scientist* helped us complete the experiment.

scuffle [skuf′əl] *v.* **scuffled, scuffling** To fight in a mixed-up way: The boys *scuffled*, but they made up right away. *syn.* fight

secretary [sek′rə·ter′ē] *n., pl.* **secretaries** A person who writes letters, takes messages, and does other office jobs: My *secretary* will tell you what time to come. ■

series [sir′ēz] *n., pl.* **series** A number of things coming one after the other: I went to a *series* of plays.

shoemaker [shoo′mā′kər] *n., pl.* **shoemakers** A person who makes and fixes shoes: I must take my brown shoes to the *shoemaker* because they have a hole. *syn.* cobbler ■

signal [sig′nəl] *v.* To tell that something is coming: Some street signs *signal* danger.

sixth [siksth] *adj.* Next in order after the fifth: Alex is in the *sixth* grade.

snooze [snooz] *n., pl.* **snoozes** A short sleep; nap: The baby had a *snooze* in the carriage. *syns.* nap, sleep

space liner [spās′ lī′nər] *n., pl.* **space liners** A large spaceship that carries passengers: Someday we may be able to travel to Mars on a *space liner.*

spice [spīs] *n., pl.* **spices** A plant substance used for flavoring food: We added *spices* to the chicken to make it taste good. *syn.* flavoring

square [skwâr] *n., pl.* **squares** An open part of a town or city where people can gather: I will meet you in the town *square* under the oak tree.

stow [stō] *v.* **stowed, stowing** To put in or pack in: I *stowed* my things in the boat's cabin.

straggle [strag'əl] *v.* **straggled, straggling** To fall behind: A few children *straggled* behind the line. *syn.* lag

strand [strand] *n., pl.* **strands** A single thread, wire, or the like: Some *strands* of hair hung in front of her eyes.

sulk [sulk] *v.* **sulked, sulking** To be in a bad mood and show it: Kevin *sulked* when he didn't get his own way.

supernova [sōō'pər·nō'və] *n., pl.* **supernovas** or **supernovae** A star that explodes, getting very bright for a short period of time: Most people have never seen a *supernova.*

surround [sə·round'] *v.* **surrounded, surrounding** To be around something on all sides: We were *surrounded* by water. *syn.* encircle

system [sis'təm] *n., pl.* **systems** An orderly plan or way of doing something: My sister and I have a *system* for doing our jobs.

T

tablet [tab'lit] *n., pl.* **tablets 1** A thin, hard surface used for writing on (used in colonial times): Sabrina wrote her spelling words on her *tablet.* **2** A pad of paper ■

a	add	o	odd	oi	oil
ā	ace	ō	open	ou	pout
â	care	ô	order	ng	ring
ä	palm	ŏŏ	took	th	thin
e	end	ōō	pool	th	this
ē	equal	u	up	zh	vision
i	it	û	burn		
ī	ice	yōō	fuse		

ə = { a in *above*   e in *sicken*   i in *possible*
 o in *melon*   u in *circus* }

taunt [tônt] *v.* **taunted, taunting** To make fun of or tease: Lee *taunted* his little brother by calling him a baby. *syn.* tease

telegraph [tel'ə·graf'] *n.* A machine used to send and receive messages over the wires or by radio: The *telegraph* was down, so we could not get in touch with our family.

tenderhearted [ten'dər·här'tid] *adj.* Thoughtful of others: Curt was so *tenderhearted* that he couldn't say no when someone asked for help. *syns.* soft, softhearted

thirteenth [thûr'tēnth'] *adj.* Next in order after twelfth: Next Tuesday is Maria's *thirteenth* birthday.

trickle [trik'əl] *v.* **trickled, trickling** To move very slowly, drop by drop: The water finally began to *trickle* out of the pipe. *syns.* drip, leak ■

tropical [trop'i·kəl] *adj.* Of the hot, humid parts of the earth: Florida's weather is often *tropical. syn.* hot

trot [trot] *v.* **trotted, trotting** To move between a walk and a run: The dog *trotted* along while Jeremy rode his bicycle.

turpentine [tûr'pən·tīn'] *n.* A liquid used for cleaning and thinning paint: Use the *turpentine* to clean those paint brushes.

U

universe [yoo'nə·vûrs'] *n.* All that exists, including the planets, stars, and space: Earth is just a small part of the *universe.*

V

valve [valv] *n., pl.* **valves** A device that controls the movement of a liquid or a gas: The water couldn't get through the pipe because the *valve* was closed.

W

washboard [wäsh′bôrd′ *or* wôsh′bôrd′] *n.*, *pl.* **wash-boards** A board with a rough surface used to rub clothes clean: You will have to scrub those pants on a *washboard*.

water-barrel [wö′tər·bar′əl] *n.*, *pl.* **water-barrels** A large container for collecting rainwater: Our *water-barrel* was full.

wax paper [waks′pā′pər] *n.* Paper that has been treated with wax to make it waterproof: My sandwich is wrapped in *wax paper*.

whelk [(h)welk] *n.*, *pl.* **whelks** A sea animal with a shell that is spiral-shaped.

The *whelk* lay on the beach. ■

whistle [(h)wis′(ə)l] *n.*, *pl.* **whistles** A device that makes a shrill sound, often used as a warning: Lupe blew the *whistle*, and we got out of the way.

wicked [wik′id] *adj.* Very bad: The *wicked* pirate robbed ‘the ship. *syn.* bad

a	add	o	odd	oi	oil
ā	ace	ō	open	ou	pout
â	care	ô	order	ng	ring
ä	palm	o͝o	took	th	thin
e	end	o͞o	pool	th	this
ē	equal	u	up	zh	vision
i	it	û	burn		
ī	ice	yo͞o	fuse		

ə = { a in *above* e in *sicken* i in *possible*
       o in *melon* u in *circus*

Photographs

Key: (t) top, (b) bo

Page iii, HBJ Phot
T. Zimmermann/F
Whitehouse; 73, H
Lefever/Grant Heil
Friedman; 199(b),
202(t), W. H. Hod
HBJ Photo; 223, La
Thompson/Stills, Ir
H. Armstrong Rob
Arnold/Old Sturbri

Illustrators

Lynn Adams: 31, 12
136–141; Carolyn Ew
Kaaren Lewis: 134–1
Michael O'Reilly: 11
Lane Yerkes: 178–18
Cover: Bob Pepper